The Confidential
Memos of I.M. Vested

The Confidential Memos of I.M. Vested

An Exposé of Corporate Mismanagement by a Senior Executive in a Major American Company

Harcourt Brace Jovanovich, Publishers
New York and London

Requests for permission to make copies of any
part of the work should be mailed to: Permissions,
Harcourt Brace Jovanovich, Inc., 757 Third Avenue,
New York, N.Y. 10017.

Library of Congress Cataloging in Publication Data
Vested, I. M.
    The confidential memos of I. M. Vested.

    Includes index.
    1. Management—United States.
    2. Corporations—United States.
    I. Title.   II. Title: Corporate mismanagement
in America.
HD70.U5V43   658.4′00973   81-47558
ISBN 0-15-193072-4   AACR2

Printed in the United States of America

First edition

B C D E

Contents

Foreword

The Confidential Memos of I. M. Vested will be a controversial book. As Dean of one of the nation's largest business schools, I am particularly aware of the need for straight talk on the problems and challenges facing corporate America in the 1980s and beyond. The confidential memos in this book should have been sent. In a sense they are being sent now. It is still not too late. American businesses can turn themselves around if corporate executives will wake up to the all too common abuses described in these memos.

The corporation described in this book cannot be named. In fact, the name and even the type of corporation is irrelevant to the purpose of the book. The mismanagement described can and probably does affect almost every type of industry and large corporation in America today.

A properly run major corporation should draw on the principles taught in our business schools and the kind of experience that I. M. Vested gathered while on the firing line for over thirty-five years. This is a book that I am pleased to recommend to all students and practitioners of American enterprise. Every corporation in America may be guilty of at least one of the abuses mentioned in this book. By studying and reflecting on tendencies and attitudes prevalent in this all too real corporation, every member of the business community can improve both his or her company's image and its balance sheet.

Despite the seriousness of the subject, these memos have

obviously been written to entertain while they educate. In a sense, eleven years of corporate history have been condensed into this slim book. It is a remarkable insight into not only the nature of American business in the 1970s but also the political and social world of that turbulent decade.

The Confidential Memos of I. M. Vested will be referred to again and again as we try to understand what went wrong with the American dream of the private enterprise system. I congratulate Mr. Vested and his publisher for their courage in presenting these sometimes stinging but always essential criticisms of big business in America.

William R. Moeckel
Dean, School of Business Administration
Miami University

Author's Preface

Many American corporations have become old, fat, tottering, and lazy. The changing of the guard from founding families to self-styled professionals has left too many of them out of leadership gas. They lack the management stamina to withstand the attacks of government bureaucrats, social demagogues, and foreign corporations. Our free enterprise system could be at stake and with it the American way of life.

Announcements that American corporations are in financial difficulty are appearing at an increasing and alarming rate. The reasons cited are: severe competition, foreign imports, labor union demands, government intervention, changing technologies, inflation, and taxes. Undoubtedly, some or all of these are culprits in each instance of financial problems, but the real cause—poor, inexperienced management—is rarely, if ever, mentioned and never admitted.

Poor management must be blamed. Too many times, successful founding families turned the reigns over to "professional managers" only to learn that they were not professional. As the companies grew, from sheer momentum for a while, and in many cases became multinational, the professional managers hired and promoted employees on the basis of association instead of qualification. They built and permitted others to build pyramids of unnecessary effort and people; they took care of themselves financially, many times at the expense of others who were really the most instrumental in the company's past successes; and in general they spent time and money foolishly on activities only remotely related to the basics of manufacturing a quality product at a competitive cost to sell at a profit. Experienced and truly great leadership is required to adhere to those basic, simple tasks and at the same time to maintain harmony with six groups of people—customers, suppliers, employees, government agencies, the general public, and the stockholders. In many cases our corporations have lost that type of leadership.

The writer spent thirty-eight years with the same corporation—all of his professional career except for five years of United States Army service during World War II. He was chosen for the corporation's college training class during his senior year in college and rose to executive positions at the divisional and group levels. The corporation was almost forty years old when he joined it, was being directed by sons of the founder, was extremely successful financially, and was growing rapidly. It continued under family direction until the early seventies and was recognized many times as one of America's best-managed companies.

In the early seventies, direction of the corporation fell to professional managers with relatively small ownership interests. It also fell prey to the trend toward a larger percentage of outside membership on the board of directors. Less than ten years later, the corporation's financial position is severely strained, its public image is degraded, and many fine employees have departed. Severe competition and changing technology are blamed. The real reasons for the degradation of the corporation are the poor, inexperienced managers and outside board members who failed on their assignment. They were kept busy racing around from one honorary, credential-seeking appointment to another without sufficient time and energy to do justice to any of them.

This book contains many of the memos written by the author while he observed the fine, proud company taking its downhill slide. They were written in his reclining chair in the evenings or while fighting bed covers during sleepless nights. But they were never sent. The degradation that prompted the memos was particularly annoying to the writer because of his conviction that it could have been circumvented with proper management. Each of the three divisions in which he served in a top management capacity was extremely successful financially. Undoubtedly, the memos are representative of other persons' memos that were never produced in final form or sent. Fictitious names, dates, and places are used throughout the book.

Now it is the author's belief that he should have sent many of the memos and that other managers should have sent similar ones. He urges all present business managers to send their memos and he trusts that corporate superiors who receive such memos will give heed. This alone might not have saved some of the companies that are no longer in business, but it surely would have sparked a savior.

Something must be done to spark saviors to save our American corporations. Each week, the *Wall Street Journal* and other periodicals contain details or at least summaries of another corporation publishing or expecting losses. We cannot continue to let this happen. We cannot lose one of the basic entities that has played such a vital part in the unequaled progress our country has made—a country only a little over two hundred years old. We must create methods to manage our way around competition (it has always existed in some form), foreign imports, labor unions' demands, government intervention, changing technologies, inflation, and taxes. We must manage our way around them or manage to get them changed.

This nation's free enterprise system and the large corporations' roles in it have been under increasing attack from so-called do-gooders. The attackers became particularly aggressive during the latter years of the fabulous sixties when we were experiencing the longest period of sustained economic expansion this country had ever had. Our economic, educational, scientific, and social lives were grappling with the close of a fifty-year period during which accomplishments were primarily those of developing the basic discoveries and inventions recorded during the previous fifty years.

During the seventies, we embarked on an entirely new era of vast scientific discoveries and inventions, which, if properly digested by all, will provide a truly exciting and enriched life. However, not all of this nation's groups are digesting and responding properly. Corporation managers are not managing around the social and economic problems brought about by our highly developed industrial society, and consequently a dangerous amount of anticorporation animosity exists. Persons who have known nothing but the good fruits of our economic expansion are resisting the very establishment that created the good living. Although profit is no longer as dirty a word as it was, some college students are still questioning entering the business world. Self-styled intellectuals engage in such absurd activities as proclaiming a "Big Business Day" to denounce corporations for their abuse of power. Sophisticated, ambulance-chasing lawyers are creating new laws under the guise of product quality claims and are forcing corporations to bear the costs of customers' abuse and misuse of products and their ignorance, indifference, and many times, laziness. Other do-gooders are expecting and forcing corporations to pick up the tab for all costs of movements designed to clean the air or to purify, improve, or change something. But they expect the corporations to remain competitive and not to close plants. The real problem? The corporation managers have not done a good enough job of managing around the people and events or of managing to change them.

America needs men and women who will rededicate themselves and those around them to the fundamentals established by Adam Smith in his *The Wealth of Nations*, to the bases of our free enterprise system. Second, leading Americans must also rededicate themselves and our entire nation to the ideas expressed in the Declaration of Independence as drafted by Thomas Jefferson. Third, our country needs business leaders with the vision, foresight, aggressiveness, ingenuity, and business acumen of the Fords, the Edisons, the Firestones, or the Ketterings. All these are needed to reestablish the healthy system of business enterprise that is so vital and fundamental in sustaining the new eras on which we embark. Corporation chiefs must become better managers and must also devote time to civic, charitable, and governmental projects and causes.

The author hopes that the confidential memos in this book will excite talented young men and women and inspire them to enter the business world; that persons already in large corporation life will commit themselves to becoming more accomplished, responsible leaders; and that all persons will gain from this book a reassurance that the free enterprise system that made our country great must and can be sustained.

It is hoped that the memos and letters will also provide some smiles and, yes, even some laughs.

Introduction

The Slone Manufacturing and Sales Company, known commercially as SMASCO, was founded at the turn of the century by Harry F. Slone, Sr. Because of Mr. Slone's vision, vibrance, resourcefulness, and persistence, SMASCO grew rapidly from a local to an international company. It remained under his direct management until the late thirties when others he had developed were placed in command. K. W. Sailor, R. L. Jamison, E. J. Lerner, H. L. Ballenger, and J. K. Sands were the men who were ready to carry on. Two sons, Harry F., Jr. and R. V., also showed real promise and interest.

Under the very capable management of those men, SMASCO continued its leadership and financial successes. Sailor retired in 1947 and H. F. Slone, Jr. succeeded him as chairman and chief executive officer. R. L. Jamison moved up to the presidency. All went well until the mid-sixties when H. F., Jr.'s retirement placed his younger brother R. V. in the chairman and chief executive spot and Al Sample in the presidency.

R. V. Slone wasn't the dynamic leader his father and older brother had been. He relinquished too much authority to those under him, and Al Sample and Rod Sailor, executive vice-president, moved in. Rod had been following Sample in each sales division promotion for at least ten years. When Sample retired in 1970, Sailor became president.

The replacement of H. F. Slone, Jr.'s strength with R. V.'s tendency to abdicate power, and Sample and Sailor's short-term management approach caused discerning men to see trouble ahead especially because Sample inaugurated a program of replacing seasoned executives with inexperienced young men.

During Rod Sailor's presidency, his top management group consisted of four executive vice-presidents: Red Harman, sales; Phil Quinn, manufacturing; Rick Gardner, international and diversified products; and R. P. Berry, finance. Harman, Quinn, and Gardner had each been promoted so rapidly that they were at their level of incompetency. All of Berry's experience had been in accounting and finance. None of them was ready to become president when Sailor retired in 1972 due to ill health. Instead of recognizing the weakness and selecting a president from outside the company, R. V. Slone gave the position to Rick Gardner.

This appointment commenced an almost unbelievable nine-year reign. It almost ruined SMASCO. In 1974, Gardner became chief executive officer in addition to his presidency, and in 1976 he became chairman to succeed the retiring R. V. Slone.

Gardner corrected none of the ills from the Sample-Sailor era. He caused SMASCO to sink into a status quo management philosophy. Instead of the many years of vision, there was management blindness. Vibrance was replaced with extreme caution, resourcefulness gave way to ineptitude, and persistence was converted to stalling, except in one respect. Gardner was persistent in placing the blame for anything that went wrong on someone else. Some of it was done publicly.

During a relatively short period, Gardner surrounded himself with men of his own type. His executive committee included Phil Quinn, Hank Paine, Jim Foster and Willard Lawton. Gardner, Quinn, and Paine had been promoted so rapidly that they hadn't been on any high-level corporate position long enough to demonstrate whether they could actually perform.

Jim Foster, as SMASCO's legal counsel, fought some wrong battles at the wrong times. And Willard Lawton, chief financial officer, had been brought in from outside the company after Berry and his successor departed. Lawton never rose above being a bookkeeper.

The comment, "Gardner, the executive committee, and the board of directors couldn't do a better job of harming SMASCO if they set out deliberately to do so," was heard with increasing frequency. It was made with increasing bravery and disgust by hitherto loyal executives. These men, who had earned membership in the family-controlled, successful-executive group, were aghast as basic management principles and common sense were regularly violated.

The majority of the complaints cited seven extremely damaging trends: deviation from the basic activities needed for manufacturing a quality product at a competitive cost to sell at a profit, short-term point of view, hiring and promoting on the basis of association instead of qualification, promotion of inexperienced young men, an ineffective board of directors caused by too many outside members, lack of emphasis on technological advancements, and disregard for the company's public image.

Deviation from the basics of manufacturing a quality product at a competitive cost to sell at a profit is a natural, line-of-least-resistance approach taken by inexperienced and inept managers to solve problems. This is especially so in dealing with government bureaucrats, labor unions, and social demagogues. It is easy for governments to print money, and it is equally easy for corporations to print forms. Gardner and his clones (particularly Lawton, the chief financial officer he brought in from the outside) were masters at creating paperwork in a foolish attempt to cure SMASCO's physical ills.

A Business Strategies and Analysis Department was established, which did nothing but redesign existing forms and controls and inaugurate new ones. No problems were solved because the department was staffed with inexperienced MBAs who didn't understand the problems.

Instead of decentralizing the world-wide activities and thereby encouraging hourly and daily decision-making by personnel "on the firing lines," new procedures gave incapable home-office managers authority that they were not prepared to exercise. The papermill volume and salaried enrollment continued to grow as unnecessary reports, letters, follow-up letters, and answers were prepared, read, and filed. Very little of the major and necessary action was taken to correct the physical wrongs that were at the root of SMASCO's decreasing-earnings trend.

The short-term point of view adopted by Al Sample and Rod Sailor was continued by Rick Gardner. It also is a line-of-least-resistance approach taken by unseasoned men who have been on the fast-promotion track. They were never on any assignment long enough to "pay for their sins." And they never acquired the habit of assuring the long-term results.

Their thinking not only lacked healthy vision, but also resulted in gimmickry, a status quo philosophy, misdirected executive work, and a general degradation of the company's position in the industry and of its public image.

Hiring and promoting on the basis of association instead of qualification became rampant. No one nurtured the orderly progression of management H. F. Slone, Sr. had established so skillfully. Al Sample and Rod Sailor had no experience other than sales assignments before taking their turns as the presidents of SMASCO. They could see no worth in anyone but salesmen. They had the erroneous belief that any successful salesperson would be an equally successful general manager. Also, promotions in other work fields (engineering, production, finance, and so forth) during the seventies were given many times to persons in locations "from whence the promoter came."

Such unprofessional bases for assigning important corporate responsibilities is bound to take its toll. It did so for SMASCO.

Closely allied to the promotion by association infraction was the much-in-vogue concept that corporation management should be transferred to young, high-potential men and women. This might be ideal if they also had the required experience and had demonstrated their ability to perform, but only if they all departed from the company early in life. If so, an orderly progression of young managers would occur. If not, a glutted personnel chain would result.

The result for SMASCO was the loss of many, very talented senior and junior executives. The seniors who were still young enough to do so sought their rewards elsewhere. The juniors left because the positions they sought wouldn't open up soon enough.

Other unfavorable results for SMASCO were poor performance at many management levels; the build-up of a large, costly training department; overuse of management seminars; and promiscuous assignment of projects to consultants. All were considered necessary to offset the void created by replacing successful older men with inexperienced young ones. SMASCO was no longer compensating for performance. Young men were in management positions at all levels in a status of training for the future. With so many men being paid handsome salaries merely to be trained, the question repeatedly asked was, "Who is managing SMASCO?" The answer was, "No one."

Not even the board of directors was doing a good enough job of managing SMASCO. Gardner had joined the parade of advocates for increased usage of directors from outside the company. He selected persons he wanted and placed them on the ballot for election by the shareholders, who didn't join together to object. Men who had neither significant ownership interest nor experience in the industry were expected to control a management group already displaying ineptitude.

This ineffective board of directors permitted the decadence of SMASCO to continue. Personnel policies were not improved, the threat of a recall was mishandled, a barrage of unfavorable publicity was not thwarted, and approval was granted to a proposed merger that was unjust for SMASCO shareholders.

There was no evidence of management interest in maintaining the technological leadership SMASCO had enjoyed for many years. Announcements of new or improved products or processes were rare. A large, beautiful, new, and well-equipped research center had been constructed, but little was heard from it. Conjecture was that the scientists had also become papermill artists—writers of reports, letters, follow-ups, and answers.

Technological leadership in data processing also waned. Great progress had been made in earlier years, and a new, large, well-equipped data center was constructed. Emphasis, however, was on converting to new equipment—not on developing the sophisticated systems of which computer configurations were capable. Data processing managers fell prey to the status quo management philosophy. They also fell prey to the computer manufacturers' marketing ability to sell new generations of equipment without the software (operating procedures) necessary to take full advantage of the technological advancements. Gardner's reluctance to assume all the responsibilities of a chief executive officer and to accept blame as necessary prompted several bad management practices. All of them either created unfavorable publicity or decreased the number of favorable news releases for SMASCO. Executives refrained from attempting anything new if there was even a remote possibility that ventures might fail. This drastically reduced the number of accomplishments that make excellent press conference material. After all, an element of risk is inherent in almost any worthwhile project to be launched. This reluctance to hazard risks and the lack of support, in case anything backfired, also added to the status quo complex.

SMASCO's public image was degraded by social ideologists' insistence on evaluating many commercial practices against new standards and doing so retroactively. Gardner's unwillingness to accept all the responsibilities of a chief executive officer caused him to publicly spank a newly found offender. The news media's eagerness to broadcast the situation was nauseating to those who had known the "grand old SMASCO."

Gardner, the executive committee, and the board of directors abdicated much of the running of the company and left it to its attorneys. With an unexpected degree of power, the lawyers settled product claim cases even though there was no product problem. They theorized that it was less costly to settle than to go to trial. But SMASCO's public image suffered.

The lawyers also enjoyed openly battling governmental agencies and news media personnel instead of joining forces with others to achieve necessary changes in an orderly manner. Each battle lowered the public's opinion of SMASCO.

All the fussing over picayune details with no professional attention to the basic, important matters; lack of proper long-range planning; failure to appoint the most qualified people to executive positions; the ineffective board of directors; de-emphasis of technological advancements; and disregard for the company's public image caused SMASCO's downward earnings trend to dip below the baseline into a loss position. Observing the development of the horrible state of affairs prompted the author to write the *Confidential Memos* . . . They describe the illnesses in greater detail and prescribe cures—it is hoped—in a unique, humorous, and thought-provoking manner.

The Confidential Memos of I. M. Vested

Short-Term Razzle Dazzle

During the mid-sixties, the author began for the first time to deal directly with members of the corporate executive committee. He observed R. V. Slone, the chairman and chief executive officer and a son of the founder, relinquishing more and more authority to Al Sample, the president, a nonfamily employee.

The author sensed a serious management degradation developing and thus—the first memo.

TO: Mr. R. V. Slone, Chairman
and Chief Executive Officer

FROM: I. M. Vested

DATE: April 19, 1969

REFERENCE:

SUBJECT: Short—Term Razzle Dazzle

Your usual quiet opening of yesterday's
quarterly meeting and the greetings to us
were like the calm before the storm. After
your introduction of Al Sample, he strode to
the podium and yelled, "Good morning Ti-
gers!" We all responded with the usual, loud,
"Good morning!" The next question was, "Who's
gonna be number one this year?" The expected
answer was, "We are!"

Thus, the meeting continued with first Al
and then Rod Sailor staging their perfor-
mances. It absolutely reeked of the
carnival—barking, pep—rally antics that have
permeated our corporate atmosphere for the
last several years since you made Al Sample
the president and Rod Sailor the executive
vice—president. If a stranger had been able
to listen from an adjacent room, much of the
meeting, I'm sure, would have reminded him
of one of those motion picture depictions of
an early Monday morning send—off for vacuum
cleaner salesmen. It reminded me of the
humorous advice on a wall hanging: "If you

4

can't dazzle them with brilliance, baffle them
with bullshit."

Throughout the entire meeting, I couldn't
help but reminisce and realize how different
the presentation would have been had your
father been alive and in command. The agenda
would have been expertly prepared, the
meeting professionally conducted and
friendly, but almost formal and short. The
first quarter results would have been exhib-
ited, analyzed, compared, and explained. We
would have been charged with expectations
for the remaining three quarters, but he
also would have discussed his long-term hopes
and plans. After soliciting our assistance
in translating his plans into specific programs, he would have expressed appreciation
for our past contributions and then ad-
journed the meeting.

During Sample's presidency, we have been
required to ballyhoo the "100 percent Perfect Workmanship" campaign; we have ar-
ranged and attended management dances; and
we've listened dozens of times to the
statements, "We don't have problems, they are
opportunities" and "Don't be afraid to make
mistakes, you have immunity." The "don't
worry about making mistakes" phrase is a complete reversal of his "100 percent Perfect
Workmanship" game.

Al seems engulfed only in projects for
short-term profits. He resists discussing
long-range plans. He labels himself and
all salesmen extrovertish and thinks they pos-

sess great leadership qualities. Consequently, all appointments of divisional presidents and foreign plant managing directors during his tenure have been from the sales ranks. This will take its toll in the future. Good district sales managers don't necessarily make good general managers.

A professor I recently met told me of his summer project at SMASCO corporate headquarters and of his exit interview with Al. When the professor asked why Al was grooming Phil Quinn so aggressively, the answer was, "I think his ethnic background will be good for SMASCO and he's an excellent golfer." The professor stopped laughing when he sensed that Al was serious.

You are the last of the Slones to be in active management of SMASCO, and frankly, what I see following you scares me. It scares others. You surely must observe why I and many others are so concerned about SMASCO's future after total direction is entrusted to nonfamily managers. We have recently seen several fine corporations slide into financial difficulty. Let's make sure this doesn't happen to SMASCO.

I. M. Vested

6

Management Lingo

Living the first eighteen years of his life in an extremely small town left several definite imprints on the author. When everyone knows so much about everybody, no one fools anyone for very long. He learned to "tell it as it is" and to accept it as such.

It was natural that once he was in the corporate world, he quickly acquired great disdain for persons who screw up their faces when they hear profound statements but actually utter so few themselves. Rod Sailor, successor to Sample as president of SMASCO, was carrying on with the insincere lingo. He was the last of the colorful peddlers.

TO: Mr. R. Sailor, President

FROM: I. M. Vested

DATE: March 1, 1970

REFERENCE·

SUBJECT: Management Lingo

Al Sample's and your flare for showmanship
and catch phrases and the company's increased use of seminars for employees have
created a new pastime at SMASCO. Managers at
all levels are devoting more and more time
to discussing the art of management and less
and less time to actually managing. A con-
tinuance of this craze is bound to be detri-
mental to our financial future.

The instructors at the seminars rarely
teach anything new—they merely send our men
back home with new phrases. We no longer
have work projects—instead they are "game
plans." We don't have profit ideas—they
are "pay words." Instead of installing a program, everything is now "implemented." Our
managers now are much more brilliant than
their predecessors because their every move is
"strategy." Where we formerly were called
to procedural improvement meetings, we now
attend think tanks. The result of anything
and everything is the "bottom line." Without actually understanding what they are talking about, men spend hours discussing "cash
flow."

8

These are examples. With each crop of graduates, more time is lost playing around with new words and phrases for the unchanging tasks of planning, organizing, directing, and controlling.

Add to this waste the time lost by all the persons attempting to identify all the initials and abbreviations so much in vogue now, and we can't help but recognize a costly trend.

I am reminded of the young man from my hometown who on graduation from college returned an enlightened man. He took over the broom manufacturing company that had been operated successfully by his wife's family for several generations. He began installing all sorts of new-fangled concepts he had learned. Employee participation in all aspects of the business was encouraged and slogans and newly coined words were seen and heard everywhere. Employees were so involved in their new world that productivity suffered. Their appetites were also whetted for constantly increasing employee benefits. Three and one-half years later the company closed its doors. Severe competition in the broom manufacturing business was cited as the reason.

Perhaps SMASCO should put an end to the time being wasted discussing the art of management and go back to managing.

I. M. Vested

Delegation

The author took great pride in his ability to delegate and in the resulting achievements. His frequent reminder was, "If anyone is to have time to think, it must be the boss. And the boss better have time to think."

When superiors perform too much of the work, subordinates do not become trained. They also lack incentive to strive for perfection with the feeling that "the boss will handle it."

But the boss who tries to handle it all usually cannot, and then no one is performing at acceptable levels. This was the predicament at our division at SMASCO.

TO: Mr. R. V. Slone, Chairman and Chief
Executive Officer

FROM: I. M. Vested

DATE: May 10, 1970

REFERENCE:

SUBJECT: Delegation

Rod Sailor called this morning and said,
"At what hotel are you and Jack staying when
you are in Chicago on Thursday?" My answer
was, "I'm sorry, but I don't even know that
I'm scheduled to be in Chicago on Thursday." His retort was, "What the hell is going
on there? Jack just told me yesterday that
the two of you would be with the northern
stores' officials, negotiating a new con-
tract." All I could say was, "I'll check
with his secretary or with him tomorrow
morning when he is back in town."

This embarrassing situation is typical.
During the last year (the first year of Jack
Lawson's presidency of this division), we
have had an extremely vivid and disgusting
display of the inability to delegate. There
is almost no resemblance between our division's operating efficiency today and what it
was under Bowles. Hap was one of the most
proficient men at delegating that I have ever
observed. Under his direction, we had a
smooth-operating, hard-hitting team, which
met or surpassed almost every goal and in-

creased the rate of profit each year. It was a genuine thrill to be a member of the team.

Now, within just one year, all that has vanished. Because of his apparent insecure feeling, Jack attempts to do everything himself. He shoots from the hip with insufficient facts; every task he performs is a rush project; and we are surprised and embarrassed regularly as customers, suppliers, and home-office personnel call us to discuss a transaction he has tried to handle for us without our knowledge. Describing our plight as a state of confusion is far too mild. We have chaos!

We no longer have a hard-hitting team. There is no team. Jack's proficiency is dangerously low as he jumps from one subject to another and in a hurried half-assed manner carries the project to something less than a satisfactory completion. He is the inexperienced fire chief who wastes so much water pissing out the small fires that he has nothing left in his bladder when the big blaze occurs. His own proficiency is low and everyone else's is almost as bad because of the lack of direction.

National Cash Register company employees still recall a story about one of the company's first chief executive officers. During the early days of the company's rapid growth, he used a ten-inch-high pyramid to demonstrate his position in relation to the managers and employees. Setting the pyramid on its base, he touched the point at the top

and said, "This is where I am, and I'm counting on you to support and hold me up
there." Then, after upending the pyramid and
balancing it on its point with one finger, he
said, "What would happen if I tried to hold
all of you up in this manner?" It was obvious
that on that basis, National Cash Register
would tumble.

I sincerely hope that Al Sample and Rod
Sailor's mania for promoting successful
salesmen who can't delegate, into top general management positions, won't cause SMASCO
to tumble.

I M. Vested

Company-Owned Retail Stores

The company's trade sales training in the stores and districts had for many years been considered one of the best in the industry. Its reputation was so good that some competitors and others utilized it as their source of employees. The resulting high turnover caused the loss of many outstanding people. It also caused a real problem in the stores.

TO: Mr. R. V. Slone, Chairman
and Chief Executive Officer

FROM: I. M. Vested

DATE: June 6, 1970

REFERENCE:

SUBJECT: Company-Owned Retail Stores

I had another good demonstration last night
of the reason that we hear so much bitching
about the manner in which our stores are
operated.

Three other customers and I were browsing
and examining intended purchases while the
only sales clerk in view was shuffling
papers in the countered-in office in the
center of the room. She made no attempt to
sell us anything. The others left the store
empty-handed, but I carried $37 worth of pur-
chases to the clerk. I asked her to charge
the amount to my account and then, within just
a few moments, my embarrassment turned to
anger.

The clerk telephoned the central credit office for approval to charge my purchases but
was having difficulty obtaining clearance.
I took the receiver and advised the credit
clerk that I was an employee with twenty-
five years' service and had been buying at the
stores during all those years. The credit
clerk said, "I don't find your name on my
list of credit customers who have a balance

16

due us." I said, "Of course you don't. I
pay any balances every thirty days and I
have not purchased anything for over a
month." At that point, the store manager
appeared, and having heard the last comment,
took the receiver, slammed it on the hook, and
approved the charge.

Think about how much worse this would have
been if it had happened to an outside customer instead of to an employee. Think
about how many times such aggravating things
do happen to a customer. How much greater
would our sales be if the salespeople weren't
so busy with paperwork in those little offices?

Our stores have become noted for undersell-
ing, overselling, unfriendliness, incompe-
tent help, credit confusion, and constant
rearrangements. Probably the only reason we
sell as much as we do is that they are also
noted for price cutting.

Why don't we have a thorough rejuvenation?
We should cease using the stores as a
short-term training ground. The good managers and employees are promoted too rapidly
or leave for better positions; the poor
ones are terminated. Only the mediocre ones
remain. With such a parade of help, the customers never become acquainted with perma-
nent, competent store managers.

Store management should be made a career
position with excellent earning potential.
The manager should have one superior to
whom he reports instead of to all the home-
office and district specialists who find it

necessary to boss the stores because of the parade of store managers and employees.

We should rebuild the reputation our stores once had—that of quality, service, friendliness, and fair price. Then with career managers and other help that aren't continually changing, customers would enjoy the shopping as they do in family-owned neighborhood stores.

We have the real estate—fine stores in excellent locations. Why not convert them into a real asset again?

I. M. Vested

Sales Incentives

Sales personnel in many companies have for years maneuvered themselves into command positions using the phrase, "Nothing happens until a sale is made." Sample and Sailor derived maximum mileage from its use.

The author is an extremely marketing-minded, nonsales person. He insists, however, on the proper balance of sales, production, development, and financial efforts, and on an equitable recognition of those efforts.

TO: Mr. R. Sailor, President

FROM: I. M. Vested

DATE: September 16, 1970

REFERENCE:

SUBJECT: Sales Incentives

The November issue of the SMASCO newsletter
arrived in this morning's mail, and one of
the articles covered a subject that has
infuriated many nonsales employees for years.
I refer to the description of the Caribbean
cruise for SMASCO dealers and for a large portion of SMASCO's sales force. The reason for
the cruise: the 1970 sales contest was a
success.

You and your predecessor Al Sample have a
peculiar definition of success. Your favorite question is, "Did you get the order?" You don't add, "Was our profit goal
maintained?" If a monthly sales quota seems
unobtainable toward the end of the month, you
use the overworked phrase, "I guess we'll
have to sell all our desks and chairs to get
over the hump." Your idol is tonnage moved.
All sales incentives are based on it.

The contest payoff just announced was based
on tonnage moved. And, like all sales incentives, it will reward salespersons for
doing work for which they were already paid.
It will also reward when no reward is due
because of all the shipments forced into the

contest period that will be taken back as returned goods in subsequent months. On top of it all, SMASCO's profit will be down because of all the special discounts, volume bonuses, and month-end deals during the contest period.

Recognition is given to the fact that it is good practice to secure large-volume business at low profit margin for overhead absorption purposes. There is, however, a critical balance between volume and profitability, and salesmen's remuneration should not be based on that volume.

Why don't you abandon once and for all the practice of basing all sales incentives on tonnage moved? Make profit generated the criterion. It is absurd to spend several hundred thousand dollars sending winners to exotic places because they met or exceeded tonnage goals but made SMASCO less profitable.

I. M. Vested

Games with Titles

Huge sums of money were spent auditing all aspects of the company's operations. Yet, under Sample and Sailor's back-slapping management, pyramid builders were permitted and many times encouraged to steal us blind.

TO: Mr. R. Sailor, President

FROM: I. M. Vested

DATE: August 22, 1971

REFERENCE:

SUBJECT: Games With Titles

Fred Hopkins's introduction of Larry Cicero to the group at yesterday's management
meeting was additional evidence of the
questionable seeds being sown at SMASCO. Taking so much time to extoll the virtues and
capabilities of a newly employed "expert" was
unprecedented and in bad taste. Introducing
him as the director of physical distribution
added an entirely new dimension to SMASCO management. A new type of director was born.
We now have a vice-president and a director
of physical distribution.

What is Hopkins going to be doing now that
Cicero is on the scene? Or, conversely, what
is Cicero going to be doing since Hopkins
is staying? The answer is that together they
will continue to build, at a faster rate,
the empire Hopkins has been constructing.
Another new wave of home-office specialists
known as directors will now splash on the
operating divisions and impede their progress.

When are we going to cease creating positions where there is no work to be done?
When will we discontinue creating titles

for fair-haired buddies and return to the practice of employing only enough qualified persons to perform the basic tasks? The cancerous enrollment growth must be arrested—yes, eliminated if we are to be cost competitive.

SMASCO has in its ranks a chairman of the board and chief executive officer, a board of directors, a president, and over two dozen other officers and assistant officers. And now, we have a director of physical distribution. How do we distinguish him from the other directors—the real McCoys?

At lower levels we also have such confusing titles as acting managers, administrative assistants, and coordinators. (A comic recently referred to a coordinator as an executive with a desk between two expediters.) The opportunities for pyramid building with titles are limitless, and SMASCO's management has certainly permitted the opportunists to build.

We should revert to the simplest type of corporate structure possible. We don't, for example, need all those assistant treasurers, controllers, and secretaries. One of each would be enough. Such titles bestow an illusory state of importance about the actual contributions these men make to SMASCO's progress. The title "manager" would more correctly describe the performance. The number of and gradations for vice-presidencies should also be reduced.

SMASCO needs a housecleaning, and it can be

accomplished with proper decentralization
and reorganization. The annual cost savings would be in the millions of dollars.

I. M. Vested

From a Pair of Deuces to Four of a Kind

For many years, SMASCO had the fine reputation of being able to hire top-ranking men from college graduating classes. This was primarily because of its company policy of providing almost limitless growth possibilities. There were no detailed position specifications outlining boundaries within which employees were forced to operate, and there were no manuals that did the thinking for the employees.

Under this program and the resulting working conditions, aggressive people almost always knew where they stood in the competitive struggle up the corporate ladder. The company enjoyed an orderly progression of persons receiving positions of greater and greater responsibility that finally leveled off not too many years before retirement.

Deviations from the program prompted the following memo.

TO: Mr. R. V. Slone, Chairman
and Chief Executive Officer

FROM: I. M. Vested

DATE: March 15, 1972

REFERENCE:

SUBJECT: From a Pair of Deuces to Four of a Kind

We didn't play much poker at our weekly
session last night. The only non-SMASCO
member asked the question early in the
evening, "Who will replace Rod Sailor as president when he retires?" The answering of
that question consumed over two hours as the
four SMASCO men who were present expressed
their opinions and concerns.

One of the men said, "Probable management
progression is no longer distinguishable at
SMASCO. For many years, a superb job was
done in having men ready at all levels in all
divisions. Also, because of the manner in
which executives were encouraged to grab responsibility, authority, and power, it was
relatively simple to predict succession to
leadership." Another member voiced, "Yes, but
Sample and Sailor destroyed all this. They
have been promoting and making appointments
on the basis of association instead of the
highest qualification. As a result, outstanding men have been replaced with young,
inexperienced managers."

We spent considerable time discussing the

four executive vice-presidents you have in the wings to replace Sailor.

Red Harman was described as the handsome, charming, socially aggressive young man who was pushed up the sales ladder in just a few years. He is not as long in business acumen as he is in executive poise. He's a polished replica of Sample and Sailor—a carnival barker in Madison Avenue clothing. Red didn't get one vote from the group as a candidate for the presidency.

The group was unanimous in its appraisal of Phil Quinn as "the man Sample was grooming for leadership because his ethnic background is good for SMASCO and because of his golfing ability." Everyone jested about the way Al had been taking Phil to golfing tournaments for a number of years. Phil was also labeled "a stubborn bastard who is apt to bulldoze down the wrong path too long." Phil got no votes.

No one could understand how Rick Gardner became an executive vice-president in the first place. He closed one division and virtually closed another because they couldn't be made profitable. Then, he slid into a corporate officership due to an untimely death of a vice-president and the rapid movement of people that Al Sample had initiated.

The financial man in the group described Ralph Berry as "the financial wizard who has antagonized so many people that information is now withheld from him, causing him to be ineffective." I personally recounted the time Ralph telephoned me and opened the conversation with, "Ian, why the hell did you establish your own college scholarship program for employees' children? Do you think you're running the Vested Manufacturing and Sales Company instead of being part of the Slone Manufacturing and Sales Company?" After another minute or so of similar statements and questions, he ran out of breath and words and I said quietly, "Ralph, I have a letter from the vice-president of personnel, instructing me to establish our own program." He offered an embarrassed apology.

We also discussed the infighting between Harman, Quinn, Gardner, and Berry for the pot of gold at Sailor's retirement. It is laughable and sad—laughable because of the antics and sad because SMASCO won't have a prize no matter who wins. The crowning statement of the evening was, "Sample and Sailor were a pair of deuces (they weren't even good enough to be jacks for openers), and now SMASCO has moved up to four of a kind." But unlike in poker, SMASCO has weakened its hand.

I. M. Vested

Data Processing

One of the greatest jobs of overselling in recent years has been accomplished by certain of the data processing equipment manufacturers. This overselling has cost industry, government, and even school systems, millions of unnecessary dollars. SMASCO was not exempt.

TO: Mr. R. P. Berry, Vice-President
and Chief Financial Officer

FROM: I. M. Vested

DATE: April 11, 1972

REFERENCE:

SUBJECT: Data Processing

Our data processing manager approached me
for approval to send two of his men to
Washington for a week to attend an Accu-
rate Data Machines school. The sole mission
was to learn how to use a new series of computer equipment. Not only did I not approve, I
also called Dick Lund, manager of the corporate computer center, and objected to his
spending stockholders' funds to send men from
many of SMASCO's domestic locations to
Washington so that ADM could sell more
equipment. He finally agreed that ADM should
send representatives to our locations at
their expense, and he cancelled the seminar.

I don't agree that ADM should even be permitted to waste our time with representatives at each of our locations. We should
issue a moratorium on conversion to new equipment. We have permitted computer equipment
manufacturers to upgrade us from first- to
second- to third-generation computers with no
benefit to us. Our personnel have spent too
much of their time continually converting to
new equipment and languages. We still are

not using the equipment as a computer. It is
serving as a fast calculator and printer. In
an attempt to justify having sold the board
of directors on building that new corporate
computer center, Jack Stover has forced all
SMASCO locations to put as many items as
possible on the computer. Many simple
jobs, which should be done manually, are being
performed by data processing at a much
greater cost.

Data processing managers, however, should
not be solely discredited for the misuse and
stagnation. Top corporate and divisional
managers have failed. They should establish
their information needs and the desired
frequency of reporting. Using the management-
by-exception approach, only those items worse
or better than a mean would be printed. Instead of seeing high stacks of data processing
tapes all over our offices, we would have
small manageable ones.

Our managers, though, won't face up to this
task because they are reluctant to reveal
that they don't understand as much about
our business as they should. Computer manufacturers have added to the dilemma by constantly ballyhooing the speed of the equipment
instead of supplying software assistance.

Recognizing their plight, data processing
experts have attempted to appear sophisticated by creating a mystical communications air. They insist on abbreviations for
everything. But I outfoxed them recently
when I determined that WPEI means "Word Processing Equipment Inventories."

For at least twenty years, data processing people have been saying, "Some day each manager will have a TV screen on the wall of his office and a panel of buttons and keys on his desk. A mere push of the buttons or keys will flash anything he wants to know about our business on the screen." The only thing I've seen on any wall was in our data processing manager's office last December. It was a twelve-foot-long ADM tape on which the computer had x'd out the spelling of Merry Christmas!

As SMASCO's chief financial officer, why don't you inaugurate a program that will make SMASCO a leader in advanced computerization and that will save, instead of cost, us money. We surely have the building in which to do it.

I. M. Vested

The Loser Wins

SMASCO had been so completely dominated for ten years by salesmen and sales philosophies that the change to a financial man as president would have been refreshing—had it not been for his questionable record.

TO: Mr. R. V. Slone, Chairman
and Chief Executive Officer

FROM: I. M. Vested

DATE: September 17, 1972

REFERENCE:

SUBJECT: The Loser Wins

If thought waves could be automatically transformed into sound waves, the executive conference room would have resounded with "Lord help us!" yesterday when you introduced Rick Gardner as SMASCO's new president.

For weeks, employees at all levels have been conjecturing, yes, even hoping that a new president would be brought in from outside the company. If previous practices had been continued, you would have been prepared with a more qualified successor from within. SMASCO was for many years. At this point, it would have been better to go to the outside. I don't know how you arrived at the selection, but a loser ironically became the winner!

I sincerely hope that Rick can overcome the stigma of closing divisions that couldn't be made profitable, and avoid selling or closing SMASCO.

I. M. Vested

Outside Directors

Although control agencies, social idealists, and governing bodies, such as the Securities and Exchange Commission, were touting the advantage of outside members on corporate boards of directors, the author spoke openly against the trend.

TO: Mr. R. V. Slone, Chairman
and Chief Executive Officer

FROM: I. M. Vested

DATE: December 15, 1972

REFERENCE:

SUBJECT: Outside Directors

Yesterday's announcement that Harold
Martin, president of Better Industries,
has been appointed as a SMASCO director,
greatly disappointed me.

I know the current trend is toward larger
and larger percentages of outside directors
on the boards of American corporations. It
is the do-gooders' answer to most every big
business problem: conflicts of interest,
political slush funds, antitrust claims, or
whatever. Actually though, instead of the
trend curing any existing illnesses, it is
certain to cause new pain.

How can a Harold Martin do us any real
good? He knows nothing about our business.
In addition to his presidency of Better
Industries, he serves on the boards of seven-
teen charitable, educational, and civic organizations. Do you think he really does justice to any of these? I am cognizant of the
need for business and professional men to
assume greater roles, and I have for some
years served in similar capacities, although for considerably fewer organizations

38

aᴛ any one time. Recognition is also given
to the fact that persons have varying
capacities for work and accomplishment. It is
doubtful, though, that any man has the capacity to satisfactorily serve all the corporations, schools, and agencies listed after
Mr. Martin's name in the news release.

Let's also remember what a board of directors is supposed to represent. Business
courses in universities have been teaching
for years that stockholders choose directors
to represent their shares. The larger the
stock ownership, the greater representation on
the board.

The recent, almost fanatic drive to boost
increased outside membership on boards has
changed all that. Directors no longer represent share ownership. They are usually
selected by the board chairman who then
makes them available for stockholders to
elect. The attitude of most is, "What else can
we do?" Do you then expect that this new,
very busy outsider will be very effective? He
will fly in with his company plane, be almost out of breath as he arrives at the beginning of the directors' meeting, and then
rubber stamp what the chairman (the guy who
selected him) wants recorded at that particu-
lar meeting.

A newly naturalized citizen was visiting my
grandfather's next-door neighbor when I met
him some years ago. He was complaining
about his wife having been persuaded to purchase a fur coat and place it in lay-away. He
grumbled, "I can no understand. I pay ten dol-

lars every payday. They got my money; they
got the coat. Vot do I got? Nothing!"

If the majority of the board members are
outside and have little ownership interest,
the shareholders' lament could very well
be, "They have our money; they control the
company. What do we have?"

SMASCO should spearhead a reversal to corporation boards staffed by men and women who
know the business, who are genuinely interested in it, who have no conflict of interest, and who represent the ownership.

I. M. Vested

Decentralization

The constant growth of corporate headquarters and increasing centralization, with a resulting inflexibility and creeping paralysis at the operating divisional level, aggravated the author. He urged stripping down to fighting weight and decentralization at every opportunity.

TO: Mr. R. A. Gardner, President

FROM: I. M. Vested

DATE: April 19, 1973

REFERENCE:

SUBJECT: Decentralization

    The stringent controls that SMASCO places
on the executives at the divisional levels
embarrassed me again this morning. I am
the Industrial Division Chairman for the 1973
United Way Campaign and had a breakfast
meeting with the general campaign chairman.
When he asked how much our company would contribute toward luncheon and dinner meeting
expenses, my answer had to be, "I'll give you
that figure after I secure home-office
approval."

    We are still attempting to operate world-
wide SMASCO with the original concepts used
when it was a small company having only a
couple of plants. The growth in size and
number of home-office departments considered necessary to control the dozens of divisions and subsidiaries around the world is
staggering. This concern prompted me to have
my secretary scan the home-office telephone
directory and prepare a list of all the
home-office departments. There are 127! This
is absurd. A quick review revealed that by
combining similar activities and eliminat-
ing some because of their duplication of

effort, the number could be reduced to
twenty-eight departments.

It doesn't take a genius to calculate that
the elimination of ninety-nine managers plus
ninety-nine secretaries would save SMASCO
at least $6 million annually. Add to that the
savings we could make in the divisions if
we didn't have all the home-office "experts"
badgering us, and the reduced cost could be
well over $8 million.

With proper decentralization, corporate
headquarters should consist of only the corporate officers and staffs needed to con-
duct and be responsible for overall planning,
organizing, leading, and controlling. It
should almost be a quiet retreat instead of
the huge, roaring, and wasteful home office
jungle it is. Emphasis should be on planning
for maintaining the company's proper and most
desirable position in the economic, educational, scientific, and social worlds. The
responsibility and authority for day-to-day
operations of SMASCO should be assigned to
the executives of each division. This would
place the work where it belongs, would provide
a steady stream of experienced executives
for corporate officerships, and would
strip SMASCO down to fighting weight.

The subject reminds me of an observation my
father made in the late fifties about the
company with which he had been associated
for almost forty years. In the twenties, the
company had 140 clock-card workers, three
factory superintendents, eighteen engineers,
a president, and three office personnel. In

the late fifties, there were still about 140
workers, three superintendents, eighteen engineers, but twenty—two in the offices.
The company had become sophisticated
report—wise. It apparently also became noncompetitive because I read several years
later (my father was no longer living to be
aggravated by it) that his beloved company had
been acquired by another manufacturer.

Why don't you clean house so that we can
withstand the attacks of some other company's attempts to acquire SMASCO?

I. M. Vested

Status

After the need for financial remuneration or resource is satisfied, almost all persons work toward power, prestige, position in society, status, or however we wish to describe it. Recognition of this basic human drive, with an organized program, can result in corporate harmony and additional profit.

TO: Mr. R. A. Gardner, President

FROM: I. M. Vested

DATE: January 9, 1974

REFERENCE:

SUBJECT: Status

Your opening of yesterday's meeting with
that insincere smile, your reading of the
entire message including "Good morning,"
and your closing statement, "We're all in this
business together," for some reason
nauseated me more than usual. We are not all
in this business together; we are different.
The people at SMASCO expect differences,
they expect status symbols, and they expect
the caste system. The comrade approach
bothers most people.

Many persons are almost as eager for the
additional status and prestige that go with
promotions as they are for the money. We
should take advantage of this human charac-
teristic instead of openly defying it. But
we should build on it in as orderly a manner as
Salary Administration builds its salary
ranges around the job-grade system.

New employees in offices find nothing ob-
jectionable about starting their careers at
a desk in the front area of a bull pen.
They expect to work their way into a succession of managers' offices and finally into

executive row. Along the way, they expect pro-
gressively to acquire water pitchers, pic-
tures on their walls, drapes, carpeting,
hall trees, coffee tables, sofas, and ever-
more-sophisticated communications equipment.

There is nothing wrong with this. Muddying
it, though, by inviting overly aggressive
youngsters into the private dining room
group, for example, before they have earned
the status, destroys morale quickly. Also,
promoting young persons into status-holding
executive positions on the basis of association instead of the highest qualification,
as you have been doing, has similar morale-
damaging results.

If everyone knew the system of status acquisition and felt assured that it would be
followed, we wouldn't have to put up with
what I call "prima donna capers." The Army
doesn't have prima donnas because a cor-
poral knows that everybody else knows that he
isn't a first sergeant. But SMASCO has them
thanks to your confusing and contradicting
personnel practices.

I wonder how much inefficiency is created
by prima donnas who worry about such things
as who answers the phone last, where a
name appears on lists, and who occupies which
seat while in an automobile?

The prima donnas, I'm sure, created and
perpetuate the famous question, "What does
he do?" I've grown so tired of it that
when I'm asked what I do, I jestingly respond

with, "I work the day shift at SMASCO."
    Let's give our employees what they want.
There should be parallel ladders to success,
one financial and the other status.

I. M. Vested

Technological Advancements

A leader in industry cannot rest on its laurels. Even a "status quo" objective results in falling behind competitors who are moving ahead.

The fear of the company's losing leadership prompted the next memo.

TO: Mr. R. A. Gardner, President

FROM: I. M. Vested

DATE: September 14, 1974

REFERENCE:

SUBJECT: Technological Advancements

Three occurrences within the last week
prompt the comparisons I'm going to make in
this letter. One, Barbara and I returned
from a short vacation on the outer banks of
North Carolina. Two, I attended a meeting
in SMASCO's beautiful, large, well-equipped
Central Research Building. And three, you and
Phil Quinn induced the board of directors to
purchase another old European company with obsolete manufacturing facilities.

There is a distinctly unhappy relationship
among the three occurrences. While on the
outer banks, we visited Kitty Hawk and the
Wright Brothers' National Memorial. We saw the
primitive little shack where so much of the
airplane was born. While walking up the steps
into the beautiful Central Research Building,
the thought struck me, "SMASCO hasn't announced a really new product or any other sort
of technological breakthrough since we've
had this building." Then, when I heard about
the other old acquisition, I mused, "When in
the hell is our management going to get off
its status quo ass and place SMASCO back on
the track of being a proud leader?"

50

Changing of the Guard

The author was having some difficulty satisfying himself about his appraisal of management abilities. His closer association with top management in recent years resulted in his having many questions he didn't previously have. He wondered whether such close acquaintance with SMASCO's earlier officers would have brought similar concerns.

There was the record, however. SMASCO had been a successful company for almost seventy years and now had a declining earnings curve.

TO: Mr. R. V. Slone, Chairman

FROM: I. M. Vested

DATE: December 12, 1974

REFERENCE:

SUBJECT: Changing of the Guard

Your announcement yesterday of the decision to step aside and relinquish the chief
executive officer's responsibilities to
Rick Gardner was both sad and disappointing.
It was sad because, even though you retained the chairmanship, it spelled the end
of a period of more than seventy years of
direction of day-to-day operations by a Slone.
It was disappointing because of the successor. Many of us had questions when you gave
the presidency to Rick two years ago. We
hoped, however, that he had outgrown his
shortcomings at the divisional level and was
ready. Now, after two years of his status
quo, picayune, motherhood-and-apple-pie op-
eration, we realize he wasn't ready.
What we don't understand is how this repe-
tition of history is telling us something
that it didn't tell you. For many years,
Rick was in top management of our small allied
subsidiary in the South. It never made any
money and finally was sold. His next assignment was the presidency of the Associated
Lines Division. Again, it couldn't make any
money and he closed down most of the opera-

tion. Then followed two extremely short
periods as president of two of our most profitable divisions (he wasn't there long
enough to evaluate his performance), and lo
and behold, only five years ago, he was
brought to corporate headquarters as a group
vice-president. In the last five years he
has held five different positions. He,
Quinn, Paine, and Broderick, who have been
following him in this rapid progression of
promotions, haven't been on any of those jobs
long enough for anyone to know whether they
can produce or not. Many of us question
whether they can.

Much is to be said for the Army's time-in-
grade approach to promotions. SMASCO followed the program until Sample's "We've
got to have young fellows" daze. It produced
seasoned, capable leaders. We need to go
back to the early sixties and pick up the
course we were on and had been on for many
years. The course was well charted, short-
and long-range plans were followed, excellent
progress was made, and there were few sur-
prises.

Before you relinquish your chairmanship
and step out completely, review how your
father left this company and what he would
expect you to do.

I. M. Vested

Youth Kick

Much controversy exists in the industrial and commercial world with respect to the merits of utilizing brilliant young men with advanced degrees as opposed to utilizing experienced and proven managers.

The author prefers a thorough program that takes advantage of high-potential people and meshes them into an orderly progression of gaining the required experience. SMASCO was not doing this!

SMASCO Ⓢ
INTEROFFICE

TO: Mr. R. A. Gardner, President
and Chief Executive Officer

FROM: I. M. Vested

DATE: February 22, 1975

REFERENCE:

SUBJECT: Youth Kick

Your setting aside of Ralph Berry as a
vice-chairman and replacing him with Cal
Rice as chief financial officer of SMASCO
astounded me. I had hoped that your assuming
of the presidency, and more recently, the
chief executive officer's responsibilities,
would stop the Sample and Sailor practice of
promoting inexperienced persons into top-
level positions.

You obviously weren't kidding several
years ago when you were still the vice-
president in charge of diversified products and you made the statement, "You don't
have to be a financial man to understand
financial statements." This was the answer you
gave me when I commented, "SMASCO has lost
the strong financial division it had for so
many years. The lack of good fiscal planning
will haunt us in the future." I suspect
there are varying degrees of understanding
anything, but the chief financial officer
should certainly completely understand all
aspects of all financial statements and reports.

58

How can Cal, in his thirties, be ready to
guide us safely through national and international financial situations? His most
responsible position at the divisional level
was as manager of accounting. He came into
corporate auditing and after only a few audits
was assigned to the treasurer's office. In
less than four years, he served as assistant
treasurer, as treasurer, and now as chief financial officer. He may be a sharp young
man on the high-potential list, but we can't
gamble with a potential in that all-important
spot. We better have an actual.

Cal's predecessors in the chief financial
post were on a first-name basis with international bankers in London, Frankfort, and
other world financial centers. Because of
Cal's inexperience, the international banking wizards are apt to chew him up.

Also, appointing Cal to that top position
at so early an age will tend to reduce the
entire financial division to mediocrity.
The older, capable people depart to seek their
fortunes elsewhere, and the very young
leave because they see too long a wait for an
opening.

For many years, SMASCO heads planned dili-
gently toward an orderly progression of employees receiving better and better jobs
until they are finally promoted in their fifties or sixties to their highest management
position. The building blocks created a firm
foundation and a powerful organizational
structure. There were very few instances of

persons having been promoted to their level of incompetence.

    We better go back to the orderly pro-
gression method and once again operate
SMASCO like a business instead of running
it like a boys' club.

I. M. Vested

Cash Flow

The growing practice of having studies made and the time wasted discussing cash flow prompted the next memo.

TO: Mr. R. A. Gardner, President
and Chief Executive Officer

FROM: I. M. Vested

DATE: May 17, 1975

REFERENCE:

SUBJECT: Cash Flow

The results of your frequent use of the
phrase, "We'll have to have a study made of
that," and the results of SMASCO's parade
of employees going off to seminars are showing
up in the most unexpected situations.

I was interviewing a SMASCO "comer" yesterday as a candidate for our marketing man-
agership. The conversation had barely
begun when he interrupted with, "Have you
hired a consulting firm to survey your market?" Not long after my answering no and trying to proceed with the interview, he chirped
in with the question, "What is this division's cash flow?"

At that point, he had already lost the job.
I took time, however, to give him the following sermon: "Our marketing and sales
managers have their own ongoing survey of the
market by working at it themselves and by
using feedback from all of our field sales
personnel. And judging from the manner in
which so many of you fellows use the words
cash flow, you would imagine some sensational
new management technique had hit the busi-

ness world. Cash flow has been around ever
since the first merchant made his first sale.
Many who use the words don't understand
them nearly as well as did the haberdasher in
the early 1900s who kept his store open twelve
hours a day, seven days a week during the
Christmas holiday season and gleefully
sang 'I sure love mine Jesus' as he rang up
another sale on his cash register."

It is obvious that many who talk about cash
flow don't understand it. Three different
formulas for calculating it are in use by
various SMASCO departments, and only one is
correct. And why should so many be concerned about it, even if they use the correct
definition? There are sufficient other mea-
surements in use for determining whether a
general manager, a sales manager, or a production manager, for example, is doing a good
job.

The treasury department personnel who provide the funds and the executive committee
members who allocate them are the persons
who are and should be concerned with cash
flow. They understand how net income, depreciation, changes in working capital,
changes in accruals, disposition of property,
intercompany activities, deferred taxes,
capital expenditures, and changes in other assets and reserves are all involved.

There is no doubt that most persons who sit
around talking about cash flow are wasting
SMASCO's time. It is another glaring example of how our management has drifted away
from the basics of running a company.

And this, Rick, is my sermon to you: "Insist that all employees get back to work, make their own studies and improvements, and create cash flow—not talk about it!"

I. M. Vested

Office Copiers

Sometime soon, company presidents will begin discussing the high costs of office copiers during their country club get-togethers. One or more of them may even order a return to the use of carbon copies.

TO: Mr. R. A Gardner, President
and Chief Executive Officer

FROM: I. M. Vested .

DATE: June 5, 1975

REFERENCE:

SUBJECT: Office Copiers

    We were tempted to call your office yester-
day and ask you to fly out here, rent a
helicopter, view our plant and office
buildings from the air, and then, as president, declare it a disaster area. All three
of our office copiers were inoperative. Our
secretaries and even some of the men haven't
been so distressed since our warehouse fire
three years ago.

    Most of our secretaries are relatively
young, and I don't believe they know about
carbon paper. With the copiers down, our
paper mill came to a halt. Even though we are
proud of our system of writing very few
letters to each other, we generate bushels of
paper answering headquarter's letters and
forwarding reports to dozens of its various
departments.

    As soon as a letter or report is typed, the
secretary heads for a copier. She invariably
makes copies for more people than she
should and then makes a couple extra. And she
usually must stand in line to wait her

turn. Adding the third copier a year ago
didn't solve the problem--we augmented the
number of copies we make! You see, each re-
cipient of a copy then has copies made for almost everyone in his department.

The advent of the copier is one of the
worst plagues that has stricken the modern-
day business world. We've had to purchase
additional filing cabinets and dead-file
floor-space areas have had to be increased.
Copies of trade secrets and confidential data
find their way much more easily into brief-
cases and then into home files of aggressive
persons who protect themselves against the
time when they may leave the company.

A few years ago, our division was under a
court order to permit a plaintiff's attorneys to peruse our files almost at will.
After the ordeal was over and freedom was re-
stored, we ordered a housecleaning. We destroyed every piece of paper that would not
have existed if the company's policy for retention and destruction of records had been
followed. Now, after just twenty-four months
of people standing in copier lines, we are
issuing the order again.

I suggest you assign a two-pronged project
to the systems and procedures specialists.
First, they should review and revise the
record retention and destruction policy. I
scanned it this morning and I am sure it is
overly protective. Second, they should survey
each SMASCO office and eliminate the need for
and preparation of every piece of paper not

absolutely needed to produce a quality product at a competitive cost to sell at a profit.

In accomplishing this project, they could probably recommend that we trade in at least half of our copiers for shredders.

I. M. Vested

Youth Kick Number 2

The resignation of a top young official, just a few months after his election, provided this next opportunity.

TO: Mr. R. A. Gardner, President
and Chief Executive Officer

FROM: I. M Vested

DATE: July 10, 1975

REFERENCE:

SUBJECT: Youth Kick Number 2

Less than five months ago, I wrote you expressing astonishment at Cal Rice's appointment to the chief financial officer post.
Now that he has resigned and left the company,
are you beginning to see the instability
that Sample, Sailor, and you create by promoting inexperienced young people too soon?

With such high-level changes happening so
quickly, what do financial analysts think of
us? What does the investing public think
of us? What can anybody think of us?

I. M. Vested

Lawyers

The spiraling cost of litigation will one day, not too far in the future, make many American corporations noncompetitive with foreign manufacturers. It could even produce financial collapse to some companies considered invincible just a few years ago.

The increasing number of cases is due primarily to the fact that weak, inept managers have been listening too much to lawyers. It is also due to the manner in which lawyers work with each other, with potential clients, and with the judicial system.

The trend was too evident at SMASCO.

TO: Mr. R. A. Gardner, President
and Chief Financial Officer

FROM: I M. Vested

DATE: February 9, 1976

REFERENCE:

SUBJECT: Lawyers

You have emphasized so often that you won't
rescue us if we get into trouble that SMASCO
executives are afraid to move without
first checking with the law department. They
have attorneys at their elbows in almost
every transaction they handle, and the results
are not good.

Joe Rounds called me from Los Angeles today
to advise that he had settled the Baird case
out of court for $75,000. I was furious!
The accident was no fault of ours, there was
no product failure, and all evidence was in
our favor. The abuse of the product by a local
serviceman and misuse by the customer created
the problem. This was another glaring example of how you are encouraging our lawyers to
take over the management of our company.

When I disagreed with Joe about the decision, his answer was, "It would cost a hell
of a lot more to defend the case in court,
and because the local serviceman has practi-
cally no net worth, the jury would expect
big SMASCO to pick up the tab."

72

Settling out of court is a self-feeding cycle. Ambulance-chasing lawyers taking cases on a percentage basis induce clients to sue us because they know we will settle. Each settlement makes us more vulnerable to the next. Over a period of time, the frequency and number of settlements causes the public and the government bureaucrats to believe that there actually is something wrong with our products. All that is wrong is the current concept that wealthy corporations should pick up the tab for all misuse, abuse, indifference, ignorance, and laziness. We absorb the cost under the fallacious conception that it is cheaper to settle than to go to trial. For any one case, that may be a correct decision, but in total, it is creating a horrendous legal cost and a damaging image.

It's a damn shame we have permitted lawyers to bring about such a state of affairs in the commercial world. Of course, our management in recent years should also be blamed for departing from Mr. Slone, Sr.'s reference to the use of attorneys. He was quick to say, "I'll run the company, and when I get into trouble, I'll expect lawyers to get me out of it."

We must reestablish the responsibility for running the company, put it where it belongs, and stop the cancerous legal growth and strangulation. In almost every case they handle, our house and outside attorneys sow seeds for further cultivation by them later. Witness the "duty to warn" law.

We now are expected to anticipate each possible act of misuse or abuse of our products and place a warning label on the package. It won't be long before the warnings will have to be in two or three languages, and then we'll have to enlarge our products to make room.

In discussing this subject with our chief legal counsel recently, I said, "Jim, if I ever foolishly pour a couple of cocktails into an empty stomach and have an automobile accident, I will sue the distillery for not having warned on the label,'Don't drink too much.'"

We have so many lawyers sitting around in meetings almost laughing about our problems (many of them created by their own ineptitude) that it is pitiful. When I see them having their frequent luncheon meetings, having fun with our problems, and charging their checks plus a markup to us, I refer to it as another "legal holiday."

During my childhood in a small midwestern town, the only lawyer almost starved until he convinced a buddy of his, also an attorney, to move into our town. After that, they both prospered.

Today's lawyers are creating law, causing and extending problems, and sending us the bill. Since they don't know enough about our business, they expect us to take them by the hand. This is referred to as the "discovery period."

I propose a period during which you discover that as chief executive officer, you

are being paid to take full responsibility
for our company in the commercial world. Stop
protecting your ass and start running the
company properly. We should fire all in-house
lawyers and close all law schools for at
least ten years.

There is still much to be said for a
genuine handshake

I M. Vested

Financial Managers

The branding of financial people as bean counters, pencil pushers, and shiny-assed clerks is truly earned by many in the profession.

The author reminds accountants, credit personnel, tax experts, and auditors, at every opportunity, to become more aggressive in placing their best foot forward.

TO: Mr. R. A. Gardner, President
   and Chief Executive Officer

FROM: I. M. Vested

DATE: June 3, 1976

REFERENCE:

SUBJECT: Financial Managers

Our division controller, Al Green just returned from the three-day, financial manager's conference hosted by Willard Lawton. This was the first such meeting he has
held since you brought him in from the outside eight months ago to be SMASCO's chief financial officer. Judging from Al's description of him, we can see why you chose him.
He, like you, is an administrator, not an
executive. He enjoys fussing around with
paper, stalling, making studies, and avoid-
ing basic decisions.
    Al and I hoped that he would return armed
with the details of a dynamic program that
you and the board of directors had inaugurated to reverse SMASCO's decreasing earnings
trend. What he brought back was a dream
turned nightmare. His first comment was, "God
help us, here we go again."
    Al's second statement was, "We're going to
try to correct SMASCO's illnesses with numbers." What he learned during the three
days was:

78

1. That the recently created Corporate Business Strategies and Analysis Department, staffed by newly hired MBAs, will revise our system of budgeting and control. Much more corporate advance approval for actions will be required.
2. Forms currently used for securing capital appropriations are being revised.
3. A redesigned travel-expense report must be used.
4. Our standard cost systems are to be converted to direct costs.
5. That the financial department's objectives are:
   a. Excellent performance.
   b. Management assistance.
   c. Training personnel.
   d. Having fun.

Such a five-point program could only have been announced by someone who has never been on the business firing line. If Willard Lawton accepted the proper business responsibilites (and he certainly should as chief financial officer), he wouldn't be muddying the water by having a bunch of MBAs who don't know our business asking ridiculous questions and establishing additional unnecessary controls. He also wouldn't be fussing around with forms revision. Neither would he gamble with direct costs. All you have to do is show divisional presidents and sales managers figures that don't include all the costs, and the result is selling price erosion.

Willard's four financial department objectives revealed how shallow he is. Why stop at excellent performance? Let's go for outstanding performance! Financial managers should think and act as managers, not as assistance givers. Job satisfaction (having fun) should be a result and not an objective.

As long as there are Willard Lawtons, financial people will be called bean counters. And as long as you and SMASCO's top management spend your time and energy, along with him, counting the beans, we'll be in the soup. We all better spend our time correcting the physical things that are wrong and chart a course that will place us on the correct financial path.

I. M. Vested

Sample's Birdie

Another promotion of a man whose track record was questionable caused the author and many others complete bewilderment.

TO: Mr. R. V. Slone, Chairman

FROM: I. M. Vested

DATE: October 5, 1976

REFERENCE:

SUBJECT: Sample's Birdie

Three choices were considered before this
memo was written. The first was a normal
congratulatory note to Phil Quinn in recognition of his election as SMASCO's president. The second was a crisp memo to Al
Sample acknowledging that, in just seven
years, his golfing buddy had chipped in for a
birdie. And the third was this memo to you,
the retiring chairman and the last of the
Slones.

The note to Phil wasn't written because it
could not have contained the serious and
complimentary phrases he would hope to
read. The letter to Al was also abandoned with
the realization that, in his retirement, he
is powerless to correct the mistakes he made.
I am writing you because, even though you are
retiring completely from active management
of the company, your ownership interest may
prompt you to head off some trouble.

There are a number of us who foresee
nothing but trouble with Phil as president and
perhaps ultimately as chairman and chief
executive officer. His ethnic background and
golfing ability haven't helped him in his

last two assignments, and they won't in the future.

As president of SMASCO International, he acquired several companies whose plants were already obsolete due to technological advancements in product construction and manufacturing processes. While heading up the American operations, he failed to prepare for the technological changes also taking place in this country and Mexico. And even before those two assignments, his track record as a divisional president was certainly much less than spectacular.

Performance, however, has not been the prerequisite for promotion during the last eight to ten years. Is it any wonder SMASCO is experiencing a degenerative performance and earnings illness? Why don't you, your brother, and your nephews become sufficiently involved to assure that the illness doesn't become terminal?

I. M. Vested

Business Strategies and Analysis

The number of home-office experts continued to grow, the paper mill expansions flourished, the company seemed to be drifting, and the decreasing earnings trend was even more severe.

TO: Mr. R. A. Gardner, President
and Chief Executive Officer

FROM: I. M. Vested

DATE: November 14, 1976

REFERENCE:

SUBJECT: Business Strategies and Analysis

In a report on the company's progress recently, you made the statement, "Inflation
is our gravest problem, but we are watching costs."

That statement reveals very clearly why the
company's earnings trend is down. You, the
board of directors, and the executive committee are watching——you are not doing. And
while you are watching, others who
shouldn't have power are encouraged in their
attempts to grab it.

A Mr. Allan Kraft, whom I had never met or
heard of before, called today from Corporate
Business Strategies and Analysis Department to tell me how we should prepare our
1976–77 budget. He didn't request; he told
me!

Telling everyone what to do and how to do
it is what that crowd of young MBAs in Business Strategies and Analysis is doing more
and more. The department is relatively new, it
is staffed with men under thirty years of
age with little or no actual business experience (the only real prerequisite for assign-

ment to the department is an advanced degree), and yet they feel free to issue orders.

Only an inexperienced person, such as a
brand-new Army lieutenant, would try to grab
so much power so quickly. Their commands
also remind me of the square-dance lesson my
high-school girl friend persuaded me to attend one evening. The regular instructor was
ill, and he sent a student who was taking
calling lessons from him (a laborer who had
never supervised anybody) to call the dance
routines for him. Well--this was his
chance. He didn't call, he commanded. And
when we faltered or made some incorrect movement, he let us know that he had the authority to straighten us out.

God help us if you are expecting these
young, inexperienced MBAs in Business
Strategies and Analysis to straighten out
SMASCO. They are cluttering already jammed
communication lines with new names and for-
mats for old reports and with new reports that
aren't needed.

Their converting of our adequate and successful financial budgeting system to that
slapstick pledge week and sledge week program is unbelievable. During pledge week, we
are expected to show you and the executive
committee, with all sorts of charts and
slides, what we will accomplish in the upcom-
ing fiscal year. (I'm amazed that they
haven't authored some sort of slogan for us to
recite while saluting the committee.) And
then during sledge week, half-way through
the year, the committee is expected to hammer

us if our performance doesn't exactly fol-
low the charts.

The whiz kids have substituted dramatics
and confusion for good management and order-
liness. Under the previous budgeting policy, we submitted our forecasts for the coming
fiscal year during the last month of a
year. The first revision, with explanations,
was prepared at the end of the first quarter,
and the final revision, again with explanations, was submitted at the end of the first
half. Only a novice would hammer divisional managers at mid-year. Strikes, upris-
ings in foreign countries, weather patterns,
and so forth make the business world volo-
atile. Only the inexperienced would design a
pledge and sledge fuss and muss.

Equally disgusting are their revisions to
the capital appropriation requests, travel-
expense reports, financial highlights, directors' books and receivables, and inventory
controls. In fact, the new formula for calculating "days supply in inventory" contains
historical sales instead of forecasted sales.
Inventories are planned for the future, not
for the past.

The entire Business Strategies and
Analysis concept of having a group of
textbook experts in the home office plan
for and control world-wide SMASCO, without the
experience to do so, is bound to end in a
fiasco! Why don't you dismantle the circus before it is too late?

I. M. Vested

Capital Appropriations

The inability of American corporations to modernize their plants on a regular basis to remain competitive with foreign companies has been publicized frequently by officials of steel companies. Most other industries have been similarly affected.

A willingness, however, on the part of SMASCO's management to accept an unacceptable rate of return because of the problem prompted the following memo.

TO: Mr R. A. Gardner, Chairman
and Chief Executive Officer

FROM: I. M. Vested

DATE: February 8, 1977

REFERENCE:

SUBJECT: Capital Appropriations

You are probably due an apology for my retort at Olga and John Corn's brunch on Sun-
day. We were discussing the last quarter
results as John handed us our first Bloody
Mary and you stated, "SMASCO's business is
just too competitive." I responded with a
sharp, "Hell, I've been in the business world
for over thirty years and each year was competitive. You'll have to cease accepting that
excuse from SMASCO managers and force them
to raise prices or cut costs or both."

I was sensitive to your defeatist attitude
because we had only last week received Willard Lawton's new guidelines for capital
appropriations. I couldn't believe what I was
reading. He advised that the corporate goal
for return on assets before interest and before taxes is 15 percent. With proud and
stern language he also warned that any funds
request with a projected payout below the 15
percent would not be approved.

It is inconceivable that you, the executive
committee, and the board of directors would

establish such a minimal goal. How in the hell will SMASCO survive?

Let's take a simple example. If you and I formed a new company; leased a building, invested $12 million in machinery and equipment; depreciated it in twelve years; had an additional $8 million in receivables, inventories, and other assets; achieved annual sales of $40 million (a rather normal relationship of assets to sales); and produced a return on assets, before interest and before taxes, of only 15 percent, we would be out of business in twelve years. With inflation as it has been and is projected to continue, the $12 million set aside in the reserve for depreciation, plus the earnings, would be insufficient to replace the machinery. (If we declared a modest dividend, it would be even worse.) And if we didn't replace and modernize, we would be operating an old, high-cost, obsolete plant and be noncompetitive.

That is exactly what is happening to SMASCO. For quite a few years, we have been on a downward spiral of making a lower rate of return on new capital appropriations than on previous ones. This has necessitated borrowing more and more and absorbing additional interest costs each year. Selling price increases have been insufficient to recover the higher costs and to replace fixed assets at inflated prices. Also, processing costs have not been lowered to offset the inflated prices. Our profit trend has certainly been downward.

It will continue downward even more rapidly
if we retain the 15 percent goal. I suggest
you revoke it and assign SMASCO managers a
challenge that will keep the company alive.

I. M. Vested

Class

Properly maintained plant and office yards, clean windows, uncluttered work areas, cheerful colors, good eating and rest areas, neat dress, and shined shoes—all these inspire and promote good workmanship. Deviating from them is almost always false economy. It was happening at SMASCO.

Mr. R. V. Slone
1847 Orange Lane
Billings, Michigan

Dear Mr. Slone:
    Even though you have been completely re-
tired from the direction of SMASCO's affairs
for over a year, I beg your tolerance of
the views expressed in this letter.
    I was in town yesterday for our quarterly
meeting with the advertising people. As I
drove my rental car into the visitors'
parking lot at 7:45 A.M. (we are no longer
picked up at the airport by company driv-
ers), Rick Gardner drove in and headed his car
onto the ramp and into the executive parking
garage. That maneuver prompted a sizable
chain of thoughts that has troubled me ever
since.
    SMASCO no longer has the corporate class it
had for so many years. When we were still a
proud company (recognized world-wide as
one of the best managed), the chairman and the
members of the executive committee didn't
drive their cars into the garage and then
spend all the time necessary to walk all the
way back to their offices. They drove up to
the main entrance, left their cars for parking
by attendants, and after a quick elevator
ride, were at work in executive row. (I'm

sure they still managed the required exercise
but at more opportune times and at more en-
joyable activities.) It was rather reassuring,
particularly when I was younger, to see those
shiny new cars lined up early in the morning
waiting to be driven to the garage by the
attendants. And it was likewise reassuring in
the evening to see them returned to the
same lineup for the executives' homeward jour-
ney. This added to our feeling that SMASCO
was in good hands.

Chances are that a corporation will definitely be in good hands if its executives
practice and support certain habits that
give it class. Examples: landscaping and con-
dition of the yards around the home office,
cleanliness of windows, clocks set correctly,
courteous lobby attendants, neat offices, and
appropriately dressed employees. Add to
these the type of advertising we once sponsored and the well-managed executive dining room, and you have a picture far superior
to that which now exists.

I'm not one to throw the ball over the
grandstand, and I don't think SMASCO ever
did, but current conditions leave us pre-
cious little about which to feel proud.

Rick and the other top officers now attempt
a show of comradeship by making such changes
as parking their own cars and discontinu-
ing the directors' table. Everyone knows, however, that they haven't saved any money because their remuneration is substantially and
relatively greater than SMASCO's officers'
salaries ever were. Add the savings from the

current shoddy yards, dirty windows, and unat-
tended clocks and lobbies, and there still
won't be enough to make up for the difference. Also, our advertising, though costly,
certainly isn't as prestigious as it once
was.

An extremely damaging effect of this delib-
erate sinking to mediocrity is the resulting
lowered employee productivity. Shoddy
plant and office appearances most certainly
will breed shoddy workmanship.

Why don't you and your brother reinstate
yourselves on our board of directors and
breathe some class and pride back into the
SMASCO organization?

I. M. Vested

Dirty Linen

Minimize liabilities and difficulties and maximize assets and good fortunes. The author was taught this adage while he was still a child. He abhorred chief executive officer Rick Gardner's traits of boasting and fighting private matters in public.

A battle with the retired vice-chairman, Ralph Berry, prompted the next memo—Dirty Linen.

TO: Mr. R. A. Gardner, Chairman
and Chief Executive Officer

FROM: I. M. Vested

DATE: November 20, 1977

REFERENCE:

SUBJECT: Dirty Linen

If you were as decisive and capable as you
are vindictive and boastful, SMASCO wouldn't
be plagued with its deteriorating financial record and public image.

When you were the four-of-a-kind winner and
became SMASCO's president, you boasted like
a bantam rooster at a dinner party, "I
guess I showed that little Irishman, Phil
Quinn, that I could go around him." Yet,
just two years later, you were involved in
naming Phil as the president to succeed you.

Also, one year after you became president,
you engineered having another of the four of
a kind, Ralph Berry, elected vice-
chairman. Now even though he retired early,
you are publicly hammering away at him for
his custodianship of SMASCO's political slush
fund. The articles in last night's <u>Evening
Gazette</u> and this morning's <u>Wall Street Jour-
nal</u> were even more nauseating than the previous eight stories on your feud with Ralph.
At the risk of damaging the company's image,
you seem to love the relentless battle. You
might as well spend SMASCO shareholders'
money to purchase prime TV time, get on the

tube, and sputter, "I didn't do it." That's
how childish it is.

Other corporation chief executive officers, when faced with the problem, settled
the matter within their own organizations
behind closed doors. They also settled with
government officials. We read about them
once and then they were forgotten. Everyone
involved, including the general public, rec-
ognizes that the current spankings with respect to political slush funds is another
example of this nation's crazy mood to
judge everything by new standards and to
make them retroactive.

The stockholders are paying you extremely
well as chief executive officer to protect
their interests--not to destroy them. They
expect you to solve problems quickly and foster the excellent reputation SMASCO has had
for so many years.

I suggest you stop the fighting, minimize
our weaknesses, and spend our advertising
and public relations money to build on our
strengths. SMASCO has a long record of making
very worthwhile contributions to progress
around the world. The members of SMASCO's
founding family have their own long record of
generous assistance to many causes. Stop
marring those records!

I. M. Vested

Product Quality

The increased number of product recalls announced by many manufacturers, SMASCO's own product problem, and a vacation incident prompted the next memo.

TO: Mr. Phillip Quinn, President

FROM: I. M. Vested

DATE: December 6, 1977

REFERENCE:

SUBJECT: Product Quality

After you closed yesterday's management meeting with, "We're going to start breaking records again; we've got the guys in this room who can do it," quite a few incidents and statements raced through my mind.

Barbara and I just returned from a short trip to Florida, exploring a real estate investment. When a restaurant parking attendant there took my car and saw the SMASCO windshield sticker, he said, "You fellas better be doin' something to improve your product." After I inquired why, he continued with, "Well, it's just the number of complaints we hear and read about."

Then I thought about Jim Foster and his lawyers' too-frequent statement, "Even though there is nothing basically wrong with our product, it is cheaper to settle a product case out of court than to take it to trial."

Then came your statement during the meeting, "I will not increase our factory costs to put excess, unnecessary quality into our products." The stubborn tone of voice reminded me of a professor's quick verbal appraisal of you after a summer's research project in SMASCO's home office some years ago. It included, "stubborn, questionable executive poise, and a tendency to use nonprofessional grammar." Harsh as it seemed at the time, the old prof was right. And that took my mind directly to your launching, several weeks ago, of the campaign entitled "Ideas That Are Worthwhile Turn On Your Boss's Smile!"

Do you understand that succession of thoughts? The world, even through a parking attendant, tells us that we have a product problem; the lawyers are throwing coals on the fire by settling out of court, even when there isn't anything wrong with our product; and you won't spend a little extra money to remove all doubt. Instead of making sure that we are producing a quality product at a competitive cost, you are devoting your time to such activities as running around the country launching the "Ideas That Are Worthwhile . . ." campaign.

With recalls now in vogue, we should make certain we don't invite a mandated one.

I. M. Vested

Training

During his annual employee assessment interview, the chief engineer requested to be enrolled, at company expense, in an extended financial manager training course. In his opinion, the combination of engineering and finance would increase his worth to the company.

The author was still smoldering over the request when he received the reminder referred to in the next memo.

TO: Mr. R. A. Gardner, Chairman
and Chief Executive Officer

FROM: I. M. Vested

DATE: January 8, 1978

REFERENCE:

SUBJECT: Training

Today's mail included Mr. Teach's annual
reminder that the recommendation for my employees' participation in company-
sponsored seminars during the 1978–79 fiscal
year is due in his office on January 31.

The brochure attached to his letter resem-
bled Community College's catalogue of evening courses. Its size prompted me to have
Helen pull the training department's similar
requests for the last five years from the
files. The growth in the number of available
seminars shocked me.

We have completely reversed the employer-
employee relationship concept that proved so
successful for SMASCO for so many years.
By that concept, SMASCO was in the market of
hiring services, and employees were in the
market of selling services. It was expected
that a mutual happiness could endure. In
order for employees to be promotable, it was
understood that they would: perform their immediate assignments in an outstanding or
at least an excellent manner, learn as much

106

as possible about the tasks of others around them, read applicable trade journals and books covering advanced technologies, and take evening courses at the local universities--all designed to advance their careers.

All that has changed. We no longer expect employees to prepare themselves for promotion or to make themselves more marketable. With your constant expansion of the training department, the company has taken over the responsibility. I do not mean to say that we shouldn't undertake the training, for example, of an operator for a new, highly sophisticated piece of communications equipment. We shouldn't, however, assume the responsibility for training everyone in all aspects of business or professional life. We also should not be attempting to train everyone to become president.

Several weeks ago, Mr. Teach sent me a note to inquire if I had any employees who needed to be taught grammar. My answer was, "If they can't talk, I don't hire them."

Employees have, for the last several years, been promoted to positions requiring technological know-how completely different from that of all their training and experience. Sales managers have been appointed as manufacturing managers and vice versa, and industrial engineers have become financial controllers overnight. When the decisions of such assignments are questioned, the answer is, "He is a comer, and we want to train him on that job." Is it any wonder

that SMASCO is in financial trouble? Instead
of paying people for what they can do for
us, we pay to train them.

One of these days, an employee who con-
siders himself or herself bypassed on a promotion will sue SMASCO. The claim will be
that the company did not train him or her sufficiently. Then we will realize what Mr.
Teach taught us.

Commandants of the Army's officer-
candidate schools boast, "We produce officers and gentlemen in three months." Those
of us who survived one of them called ourselves ninety-day wonders. SMASCO is becoming
filled with three-day, five-day, two-week,
and three-month wonders. Don't you wonder
how much longer we can afford it?

I. M. Vested

Personnel Handling

Overreaction is a good indication of poor management. Emphasis on equal employment opportunity in our country during the seventies was the excuse Rick Gardner cited for a horrendous buildup in employee-related activities.

TO: Mr. R. A. Gardner, Chairman
and Chief Executive Officer

FROM: I. M. Vested

DATE: March 19, 1978

REFERENCE:

SUBJECT: Personnel Handling

Our personnel replacement requisition for
a quality control manager has been approved
(three and a half weeks after submission),
and the process of reviewing personnel folders
of potential candidates has begun. The second folder I examined contained a document
that shook me. It caused me to realize just
how far we have strayed from the basics of
employing people.

The document was Mr. Kress's psychologist's
description and analysis of the candidate.
I have never read worse gobbledygook!
Here are some of the profound statements:

"The single most appropriate decision-
making approach favored by Mr. Black would
be to consult with his superior before
proceeding."

"The job responsibilities that Mr. Black
feels are important to managers are to offer
new solutions to problems and to seek and
obtain the approval of one's superior before
going ahead."

"Successful business leaders, in Mr.
Black's opinion, consider in an equal and

thorough depth the long-range and immediate consequences of their actions."

"They are very likely, Mr. Black feels, to be interested in practical and useful matters of no apparent immediate concern."

"Mr. Black says that he favors work tasks of a very difficult or very simple nature."

"In comparison to other successful SMASCO persons, Mr. Black appears to have acceptable levels of tolerance and a need to be successful. His leadership interest seems to be good and he also appears to be good at realizing where others are coming from and at practicing empathy toward other people."

The "comparison to other successful SMASCO persons" phrase bothers the hell out of me. If Kress's analysis of Black is reliable and if Black is rated acceptable and good by comparison, then SMASCO's successful managers must be unsuccessful by most persons' standards. I object!

I also object to many of the other paper mill activities in which the personnel department engages. We must now prepare elaborate employee appraisals and performance evaluations. We complete ballots to vote for or against an employee or an outsider seeking a position. We reward mediocrity or even incompetence by complying with equal employment opportunity policies that are more stringent than necessary. The need for an employee to improve himself or herself has been eliminated by the company having assumed the responsibility to train and prepare them for promotion. Labor relations and

salaried personnel activities have been com-
bined under one head in each plant (a newly
created position), even though few, if
any, of the chiefs are proficient in both.

Despite these examples of paperwork growth
and control, desired results have not been
achieved. Employees resist accepting
foreign assignments because there is no evidence that they will have an opportunity
for top positions after their return. Also,
all the appraisals, assessments, ballots,
seminars, and accompanying paperwork have
not resulted in promotion on the basis of
qualification, particularly at management
levels. Promotion is by association. The
Southern Clique was replaced by the Midwest
Planters who have been overcome by the New
England Stars.

Such a basis for hiring and promoting is
not too far removed from a situation I had
some years ago with our divisional president who was a gregarious, lifelong peddler.
On two different occasions on arriving at
the office in the morning, I found a bartender
and a taxi driver waiting. Their comment was
"Mr. Bowles hired me last night to become a
district manager and asked me to see you." On
a third occasion, the applicant was a
door-to-door salesman whose aggressiveness
was admired by Bowles's wife.

Recently, when another promotion by association was announced, the news release
stated that the new appointee had come up
through the ranks. One of our employees de-

scribed that as meaning, "He worked one
summer in the shipping department."

Surely, the time has come to rid ourselves
of all the unnecessary and ineffective personnel department activities.

I. M. Vested

Recall Battle

Repeated, unfavorable publicity with respect to SMASCO's product was becoming extremely embarrassing for all the employees.

TO: Mr. R. A. Gardner, Chairman
and Chief Executive Officer

FROM: I. M. Vested

DATE: April 25, 1978

REFERENCE:

SUBJECT: Recall Battle

You made the headlines again last night
with, "SMASCO Insists No Recall Is Necessary."

SMASCO has carried this issue to the point
that whether or not it is necessary will
soon be irrelevant. The widespread news
coverage; the number of congressional and
other investigations, which have forced
other companies to announce recalls; and the
government bureaucrats sitting around licking
their chops won't leave you any choice. Our
history of settling cases out of court is also
against us.

A quiet, voluntary recall no longer scares
consumers. Many purchasers of automobiles
have experienced them. A voluntary recall
strengthens public confidence in a product and
doesn't really damage the company's reputation. It actually reassures customers that the
manufacturer stands behind his products.

An international leader recently fought
the news media and a branch of the government and lost the battle Why don't you go

to school on that as the golfer does while
watching his opponent putt ahead of him on
a tricky green.

You can't fight the news media and the government and win.

I. M. Vested

Approvals

The chief financial officer, Willard Lawton, continued to an-
tagonize others with his unrealistic demands and concepts.

TO: Mr. W. Lawton, Chief
Financial Officer

FROM: I. M. Vested

DATE: May 10, 1978

REFERENCE:

SUBJECT: Approvals

Our division controller came into my office
this morning like a beaten dog with his tail
between his legs. He had just had your
message relayed to him that there was no excuse for the substantial upward revision to
our expansion appropriation. You charged also
that any controller who couldn't control
costs any better than that, wasn't a controller.

Well, by the time he left my office, he was
no longer beaten. And I'm going to tell you
the same thing I told him. Any chief financial officer who hasn't performed any better than you have since joining the company
over two years ago should be removed from the
position. I'm sure it would be judged by most
SMASCO executives who know both of you that
Joe Black is as much a controller as you are or
ever will be a chief financial officer.

You haven't improved a thing since coming
with us. In fact, you have hurt SMASCO with
your philosophy that its ills can be cured
with numbers and paperwork.

Our new capital appropriation approval

120

system is preposterous. The length of time
it takes and the number of people who are
involved is ridiculous—much worse than it
ever was. Then, after the request finally
reaches us approved, we must forward each
purchase order for $10,000 or more to the
home office for a second approval of that
portion of the project. Therein lies the reason for appropriation overruns, Mr. Smart-
ass! With inflation as unpredictable as it
has been, with approval time as lengthy as it
is, and with all those home-office "experts" whittling the appropriation during the
process, it is impossible for the Joe Blacks
to prevent the need for revisions to cover
overruns.

Instead of initiating the type of phone
call made this morning, why don't you exam-
ine all of SMASCO's approval processes.
Count the number of offices each request vis-
its and note the total time consumed for
the approvals. You'll find fertile ground for
enormous cost savings. I call it fertile
ground because that is what horse manure
produces.

Judging from the past two years' practices,
though, you'll undoubtedly hire an outside
consulting firm to make the examination at
an absurdly high cost.

I. M. Vested

Pricing

The pincer-like movements of Sample and Sailor while SMASCO's financial division was weakening had given the sales personnel responsibility for pricing. With his status quo, do-nothing approach to management, Rick Gardner never took complete control.

Using the concept of "fill the plant and absorb the overhead," price erosion set in. This was another source of SMASCO's financial problems.

TO: Mr. R. A. Gardner, Chairman
and Chief Executive Officer

FROM: I. M. Vested

DATE: August 22, 1978

REFERENCE:

SUBJECT: Pricing

Our sales manager and I just returned from
New York after negotiating with our major
original-equipment manufacturing account
for a price increase to cover a raw-material
cost increase. As usual, we had been offered about 70 percent of our original request
(which was somewhat loaded because we are
familiar with their tactics), and we settled
for 93 percent.

After we signed off with the purchasing
agent, he said, "If your parent company were
as tough as you on pricing their product,
SMASCO wouldn't be in the financial difficulties we read about." He elaborated, saying,
"George Mayberry was in two days ago, and
after we applied some heat he reduced prices
12 percent."

This is what invariably happens when a company establishes the reputation of being a
price cutter It reminds me of the story
about the lonesome traveler who became a little friendlier than usual with the waitress
in the hotel dining room. He inquired if she
would spend the night with him for a million

dollars, and without too much thought she responded that she probably would. When asked, "How about twenty dollars?", she almost yelled, "What the hell do you think I am?" His answer was, "We have already established that, we're just negotiating the price."

When a company repeatedly cuts price, trying to buy a larger share of the market, it becomes known as the whore of the industry. I certainly hope SMASCO doesn't pick up that tag. Our recent bouts with the news media and the government have given us enough unpleasantness to overcome.

In the SMASCO divisions with which I have been associated, we consider pricing one of the most important tasks. We never permit salespersons to deviate from the prices established by the president and the chief financial officer without securing advance approval from those two. This forces the president and the finance man to keep their fingers on the pulse of the market. We never cut prices, but we will meet competition head-on when it is necessary to retain an account we don't want to lose. Not having bought an increased share of the market, the competition soon raises prices again. We do likewise, and then everyone is back in the black.

All price cutters should get a fresh start in the business world by joining a Junior Achievement company. There they could learn the basics of making a quality product at a competitive cost to sell at a profit. Junior Achievement won't teach them to ship

the product out of the warehouse and then go
to the bank to withdraw a few dollars to
send along with the product to the customer.

Perhaps our purchasing agent friend in New
York was somewhat out of order in commenting
as he did. Certainly, you should take heed
and insist that SMASCO salespeople sell quality and service at an appropriate price.

I. M. Vested

From Four of a Kind to a Straight Flush

It was becoming apparent to SMASCO's operating executives that corporate leadership had virtually collapsed. While Rick Gardner, the chief executive officer, and his executive committee devoted their time to trivia, SMASCO was floating as aimlessly as a rudderless ship at sea. And the board of directors, who should have stepped in, were on a free ride on the ship.

TO: Mr. R. A. Gardner, Chairman
and Chief Executive Officer

FROM: I. M. Vested

DATE: September 16, 1978

REFERENCE:

SUBJECT: From Four of a Kind to a Straight Flush

The horrible lack of leadership at SMASCO
was marked indelibly on my mind yesterday
during the hour I spent before you and the
executive committee. You approved the expansions of our Mexican plants, but what an
ordeal!

In accordance with the current require-
ments, I had all the charts, graphs, trends,
comparisons, and analyses projected on the
screen. Three times you asked the question,
"How do we know those numbers are correct?"
And twice you charged, "Those examples aren't
comparable." I ignored your questions because
I knew the continuation of my presentation
would prove how silly your comments were. The
only question that revealed any thought at
all was your, "What do we do if, some years
from now, it is no longer so advantageous
from a cost standpoint to manufacture in
Mexico?" You should have known the answer:
"We'll move the equipment back into the States
and sell the building."

Phil Quinn contributed nothing to the meeting. He made two irrelevant observations re-

128

lating to the period when he was president
of this division.

Willard Lawton displayed his usual confusion when he stated, "The changing value of
the Mexican peso isn't a factor." If the
changing values of foreign currencies aren't a
factor, why do SMASCO and other multinational corporations constantly use in their
reports the phrase, "Earnings were adversely
affected by foreign currency exchange losses?" And this statement was made by SMASCO's
chief financial officer!

Hank Paine didn't even once use his famous
phrase, "If you will please." He said nothing. I heard his insincere giggle a couple
of times, but I really just ignored him as he
sat there like a big fat puppy dog. He knew
that he wouldn't be involved in the decision
because he habitually postpones or dodges
making one. In fact, when we saw you and him
on television recently, he removed and replaced his spectacles each time you did.
But I guess making no decisions is superior
to making bad ones. It is considered by most
SMASCO managers that he should never have
been promoted beyond an engineering position
at the divisional level. Yet here he is one of
your executive vice-presidents.

The fifth member, Jim Foster, was obviously
bored with all the charts and numbers. He
was half asleep most of the time.

During that hour on my feet, facing the
five of you—the chairman and chief executive officer, the president, two executive
vice-presidents, and the vice-president and

general counsel—the thought entered my
mind, "My God! In less than ten years, SMASCO
has gone from a pair of deuces to four of a
kind and now to a straight flush. And each
time SMASCO's hand has gotten worse. I hope
this straight flush group, along with the
ineffective board of directors, doesn't
flush SMASCO down the drain."

I. M. Vested

Proposed Merger

The announcement of a proposed merger, completely inequitable for SMASCO's shareholders, and the sudden realization that a formerly great corporation would lose its identity, angered many, including the author, to an almost uncontrollable hatred of Rick Gardner and the board of directors.

TO: Mr. R. A. Gardner, Chairman
and Chief Executive Officer

FROM: I. M. Vested

DATE: December 5, 1978

REFERENCE:

SUBJECT: Proposed Merger

This is the fifth revision of this memo
in the seven days since the proposed merger
of SMASCO and Development Unlimited was
announced. Two delightful, preholiday dinner
parties kept me out of my easy chair and
kept my mind at least partially off the subject of this memo for two nights.

The announcement was an unprecedented
shocker. Those of us who have our twenty-
year watches and several diamond pins were
left with the hollow feeling of having been
sold out.

A sellout is what it is. Ever since you
have taken command of SMASCO, reference has
been made regularly to an interest in diversification. But nothing has been acquired.
And now, again using diversification
phraseology, you announce a plan that allows a
company half our size to take over SMASCO.
Development Unlimited is the one that is
diversifying—not SMASCO!

How can you justify to any of us stockholders the trading of our shares for pre-
ferred shares in the new proposed holding

company at little more than 50 percent of the current equity value? Under the proposed arrangement, the Development Unlimited shareholders, who are to receive common shares in the holding company, will acquire SMASCO at virtually its working capital figure.

I wonder how far you would have been able to develop this proposal if old man Slone were still around? In fact, I wonder if you would still be around if he were? During your earlier years at the divisional level, we sold one division and closed down another because you couldn't make an acceptable profit. And now, with the total corporation earnings on a downward trend, you plan to give the entire company away.

How can the stockholders approve the proposal at the special meeting to be scheduled? How can you possibly prepare to satisfactorily answer the questions that surely will be raised?

I. M. Vested

Compensation

Year-end management bonus letters were placed in the mails. Due to the continuing downward earnings trend for the corporation, even the profit contributors were awarded less than anticipated. A Merry Christmas?

TO: Mr. R. A. Gardner, Chairman
and Chief Executive Officer

FROM: I. M. Vested

DATE: December 19, 1978

REFERENCE:

SUBJECT: Compensation

The morning's mail delivery brought this
year's annual pre-Christmas letter from you
announcing my management bonus for the
past year.

The overworked, nauseous phrases of the
last four or five annual letters were used
again this year. In short they said, "The
company didn't do well this year, so you don't
get much."

My question is, "Will the proxy statement
this year show that you also didn't get
much?" Or will it reveal that you and your
top cronies improved your remuneration package
handsomely again as in prior years? It is
ironic. The men responsible for the company's
not doing well use the financial plight as
the reason for not rewarding second- and
third-tier management persons but find some
other basis for increasing their own earnings.

You engaged a consulting firm to study
compensation—the Lay Company. All that they
accomplished was to augment the inequities
that had already been created. Your managers,

who are actually holding the company together, are saying, "The Lay Company laid us
away."

SMASCO's executive salaries alone have
never been competitive. With bonuses added,
the total kept us in line until the last
several years. Reduced bonuses have now placed
executives in the position of not staying
abreast of inflation.

Last year, when we learned of and com-
plained about the fact that executives in
loss divisions received bonus treatment no
worse than ours, the answer was, "We didn't
want to ruin their morale completely." I
say, "If they can't make a profit, replace
them. Don't worry about their morale!"

SMASCO's reimbursement program needs revision.

                                    I. M. Vested

Don't Let It Happen

"The proposed merger must be killed and management must be purged."

This became the comment at all employee levels.

Mr. K. W. Slone
2001 River Road
Singing Woods, Virginia

Dear Kenneth:

Don't let it happen.

Why don't you and other members of your
family get some balls, attend the next
SMASCO board of directors' meeting, and
drive the money changers out of the temple?
Break up the proposed merger!

Mr. Gardner and his top management aides,
with the blessing of the board members, are
exchanging your and the stockholders'
money for their own face-saving prestige. They
have finally admitted their management in-
adequacy to themselves. Via the proposed
merger, they are ready to give the company
away so that they may have high-title positions in the new holding company. Titles, but
no power.

Because they are willing to relinquish
their power, it should be easy for you to
remove them from office, replace them with
a new, highly-qualified management team, and
save the company. Your grandfather would
expect you to do just that.

What would your grandfather think if he
knew that his grandson had left SMASCO to
pursue his own business interests? What
would be his reaction on learning that only

one Slone is on the board to represent the entire family's interests in the company? What would he do to halt SMASCO's decreasing earnings trend? To what lengths would he go to restore SMASCO's good name and to assure that its separate identity is retained?

You know the answers. Act on behalf of your grandfather, and you will also be acting in your own best interests.

I. M. Vested

Consultants

Due obviously to a feeling of insecurity, consultants had been engaged promiscuously. Employees were pestered regularly by the gatherers of information.

The office grapevine was filled with jokes, ridicule, and a mounting loss of respect for management.

TO: Mr. R. A. Gardner, Chairman
and Chief Executive Officer

FROM: I. M. Vested

DATE: February 19, 1979

REFERENCE:

SUBJECT: Consultants

When I drove into the main gate yesterday
for a meeting with Len Broderick, a guard I
had never seen before stopped me and said,
"The visitors' parking lot is filled—you'll
have to park at the north end of the west
parking lot." With snow blowing into my open
window and a wind-chill factor well below
zero, I objected to such a long walk and responded, "Please call Mr. Broderick and tell
him Vested is canceling the meeting because there is no place to park." He quickly
changed his mind and suggested that I park
laterally by the sidewalk at the main entrance. I wonder how many friends of SMASCO
have become unfriendly as they encountered the
same ridiculous situation?

It is ridiculous because most of the visitors' spaces have been occupied for many
months by employees working for all the
consulting companies you and Will Lawton have
been engaging. And it's become even worse
during the last several months. Both parties
to the proposed merger now also have representatives of investment banking houses,

144

public accounting companies, and law firms crawling all over the place in here.

I suspect all those people running around delving into all aspects of SMASCO's business are the result of what has happened to this company during the last decade. You and your top management personnel have been promoted every year or two. Also, with almost a religious fervor, you have been assigning very young, inexperienced people to positions of great responsibility. And then you became frightened. And then you called in the consultants!

The consultants are expected to help you do the job. They'll assist you in stalling if you don't want to do anything, they'll give you the basis for placing the blame on someone other than yourself if something goes wrong, and they are costing SMASCO a hell of a lot of money.

The office jokesters' joke of the year is, "We'll have a study made." Our manager of accounting, frustrated with all the questions from the fact-gatherers, said recently, "I'm going to get an unlisted company telephone number."

With your constant use of consultants and then the proposed merger, you have admitted to the world that you can't manage SMASCO. Why don't you admit it to yourself?

I. M. Vested

Merger Discussions Terminated

The family and other major shareholders apparently had their fill. The merger discussions were terminated.

1616 Old Mill Road
Clarkton, Illinois
April 26, 1979

Mr. K. W. Slone
2001 River Road
Singing Woods, Virginia

Dear Kenneth.

Congratulations! You didn't let it happen.

Today's news release announcing that the proposed merger talks were terminated was like a fresh, spring breeze breathing new life into everyone in our division and, I'm sure, all of SMASCO.

We trust that you and the other family members will now force the policy and management changes so sorely needed to return SMASCO to the strong, successful, proud company it was for so many years.

Ian

148

Strategic Business Elements

The merger fanfare was over, but the Straight Flush Five were still there and that's it—-they were just there.

The imprudent concept of curing the company's ills with numbers and reports continued to grow. A new game, "Strategic Business Elements," was launched.

TO: Mr. R. A. Gardner, Chairman
and Chief Executive Officer

FROM: I. M. Vested

DATE: June 15, 1979

REFERENCE:

SUBJECT: Strategic Business Elements

Here we go again. You have launched another
paperwork program to cure SMASCO's ills. I
am referring to SBE (Strategic Business
Elements).

We have been answering questions from the
consultants working on the project, but we
learned today that we are expected to re-
gard those three letters with great reverence
because of the totally new management concept. I'll have to say that it took the reverence of a reverend to sit through the presentation.

With great pride, Ralph Clemson announced
the program. It didn't take us long to
realize, however, that it isn't a new management technique. The only thing new about it
is the placing of all the important and
confidential details regarding our products
and programs on one large piece of paper. And
that is the aspect to which I object.

Within a relatively short period of time,
the world will know all about us. There will
be no secrets. Every employee who has the
slightest thought of changing companies some

150

day will carry copies home. Instead of the letters SBE designating Strategic Business Elements, they could well be crying out, "Secrets Broadcast Everywhere."

Such freedom with highly confidential information is a complete reversal of one of the basic policies, which, I'm sure, was instrumental in SMASCO's growth and success. Unit costs and profits, for example, were guarded closely, to be used by only a few who needed to know. Only the people involved knew of major programs before they went into effect. We surprised competitors time and again. We defined, calculated, and worked with all the same information we are now asked to place on one sheet of paper. But we didn't invite theft by making it so easy to steal.

The primary goal, I'm sure, is to make it easy for persons who were promoted too soon to become comfortable in their assignments.

I can't imagine that you and the board of directors would continue to permit this cancerous growth of paper and numbers games that tend only to protect ineffective and unproductive managers.

I. M. Vested

Misdirected Executive Work

No plans or programs were announced for the turnaround of SMASCO. Employees at all levels were complaining, "Gardner is killing time until his retirement, fussing around with the unimportant—an easy out for managers with relatively little ownership interest."

TO: Mr. R. A. Gardner, Chairman
and Chief Executive Officer

FROM: I. M. Vested

DATE: July 10, 1979

REFERENCE:

SUBJECT: Misdirected Executive Work

It is becoming almost impossible to remain
a loyal SMASCO executive. How can we comment
on the statement heard more and more frequently, "Gardner has a built-in tolerance for
losses. He had them himself and got promotions, and he promotes instead of replaces
executives who can't make a profit."

My response usually is, "Don't jump; the
situation is bound to improve." What I'm actually thinking each time is, "It's bound
to get better—how could it get any worse?"

Today, I learned it had gotten worse. While
sitting in Jim Foster's outer office waiting
to be beckoned in, I overheard two secretaries bitching about how you are spending your
time approving salary increases for low-
level managers and assigning secretaries to
executives. They laughed about your devoting
time to it, but they were angered over some
of your decisions.

Instead of laughing or being angry, I
wanted to vomit! At a time when the very future of our company could be threatened,
shouldn't you be concerned with:

a. Turning our losing divisions around or disposing of them?
b. Maintaining product quality?
c. Replacing ineffective and incapable executives and managers?
d. Taking the bull by the horns and reversing the trend in product liability claims and law suits?
e. Keeping abreast of international developments and world supply-and-demand situations?
f. Maintaining technological leadership?
g. Retaining our strength in supplies and sources of raw materials?
h. Determining world-wide marketing strategies?
i. Diversification.
j. Assuring the long-term profitability of SMASCO?

One of your favorite comments in speeches is, "Don't work harder—work smarter." Why don't you practice what you preach?

I. M. Vested

Sample's Dead Duck

A second favorable news release appeared. Phil Quinn took
early retirement.

1616 Old Mill Road
Clarkton, Illinois
July 20, 1979

Mr. K. W. Slone
2001 River Road
Singing Woods, Virginia

Dear Kenneth:

It is wonderful to write to you again expressing gratitude. Phil Quinn's announcement today that he is resigning from the presidency of SMASCO and as a director is beautiful news. Sample's golfing buddy's birdie days are over and he's now a dead duck! He bogied, as many of us knew he would.

His departure definitely indicates that you and other Slone family members are becoming active. The cessation of merger plans three months ago, the resignation from the board of an outside director who was one of those who encouraged the merger, and now Phil's departure from the company are developments many of us have been awaiting.

As I view it, we now have one down and four to go! The money changers still to be driven out are Gardner, Lawton, Foster, and Paine. The search committee appointed to replace Quinn with a capable executive from outside the company may as well broaden their search and locate successors for the other four.

We would not have to go to the outside if appointments had been made on the basis of

158

qualification instead of association. A
number of those who were bypassed sought and
received better employment elsewhere. The
board of directors has permitted a serious de-
generation of our management talent during
the last seven or eight years.

While I was attending a Chamber of Commerce
dinner meeting several months ago, the man
to my left (the president and principal
owner of a construction company) wanted to
discuss SMASCO. He said, "It is inconceivable to me how Gardner and Quinn acquired the
two top spots. I know them both very well. I
play golf with them; they are fine fellows
as friends, but as heads of world-wide SMASCO,
no, no, no." And he kept shaking his head
from side to side.

I hope the board will now be strengthened
by more family members coming back and joining you. We certainly need more ownership
represented to correct our management weakness.

Thinking about the situation with which the
Slone family has been confronted reminds me
of the quotation on a wall plaque I saw
recently. It said, "It is difficult to soar
like an eagle when you are working with
turkeys."

I. M. Vested

Welcome the New President

A new president from the outside is welcomed.

TO: Mr R. I. Palmer, President

FROM: I. M Vested

DATE: September 10, 1979

REFERENCE:

SUBJECT: Welcome

Welcome to SMASCO and congratulations on assuming the presidency.

Your comments after Gardner introduced you to the group yesterday were refreshing. It was a pleasant return to earlier days to hear you admit that a mistake might be made occasionally and to also assure us that corrective action would be taken immediately. The announcement that you already have plans to make SMASCO healthy again provided the exhilaration we needed.

Making SMASCO healthy will be difficult, but not impossible. After nearly seventy years of unusually capable management, we fell prey to a little over ten years of extremely poor management. It was shocking to observe how quickly a small group of inept officers and an ineffective board of directors could place a strong company on the financial skids.

We trust your plans will take SMASCO off the skids quickly and build on the many good blocks still remaining. One of those blocks is our division, and you have our commitment to continue to contribute above-average financial results.

I. M. Vested

Decisions

The new president, Palmer, started making his moves to re-structure the company and turn it around. Several plant closings and the deactivation of one division were announced. Although Palmer was not yet the chief executive officer, it was obvious to other SMASCO managers that the Slone family had given total power to him.

TO: Mr R. I. Palmer, President

FROM: I. M Vested

DATE: February 20, 1980

REFERENCE:

SUBJECT: Decisions

The news release today announcing the closing of the Mid-States Division and other
SMASCO plants stunned many people. I'm
sure it revealed to discerning persons the financial depth to which SMASCO has fallen,
but it also loudly proclaimed that SMASCO now
has management who can make major decisions
and make good ones.

Less than a year ago, but before you arrived, the Carlton Division was merged into
the Mid-States Division because of the al-
leged economies. Ignoring the fact that the
Mid-States office building was already
crowded, good office space at Carlton was va-
cated. Huge relocation expenses were incurred
to move Carlton's salaried employees and
their families, and then discussions began regarding the need for a new Mid-States office building. All of this commotion was
over two ailing divisions, which you now find
it necessary to close.

This is a glaring example of the confused
thinking that has caused the cash hemorrhaging now plaguing you and SMASCO.

Other instances of confused thinking and

the resulting cash hemorrhaging are: the acquisition of technologically obsolete plants; launching a new plant with none of the management team having any experience in manufacturing the products involved (the brilliant concept was, "We don't want any of the bad habits of existing plants to be transferred."); and of course, the horrendous recall battle that ended finally in much more expense and unfavorable publicity than if it had been conducted earlier and more quietly.

Those horrible mistakes and many more during the last ten or twelve years are apt to be the bases for case studies in leading graduate business schools for many years. They may well be entitled, "The SMASCO Fiasco—How Not to Manage a Corporation."

Five of the men responsible for the fiasco: Sample, Sailor, Harman, Quinn, and Foster are already gone. Three of the greatest offenders, Gardner, Lawton, and Paine, are still around. I sincerely hope they won't impede your progress in taking additional corrective action.

Good luck!

I. M. Vested

Family Coming Back

A third and extemely favorable news release appears. A family member, Lawrence Slone, rejoins the board of directors. The next letter contains the challenge.

1616 Old Mill Road
Clarkton, Illinois
February 25, 1980

Mr. Lawrence Slone
727 Mulberry Lane
Orchardville, Oregon

Dear Mr. Slone:

SMASCO employees, customers, suppliers,
and shareholders all join me, I'm sure, in
saying amen to your decision to return to
our board of directors. If our late, mutual
friend H. M. (Hap) Bowles were here, he
would dedicate a song to the occasion.

The announcement was surely the kind of
happy news needed by everyone involved with
our company. With the proposed merger
called off, with Quinn and Foster already
gone, and with Palmer on the scene, your
coming back on the board announces clearly
that the Slone family has had enough. We
trust you will now continue with the replacement of the remaining top management personnel
who have permitted SMASCO's decadence. We
hope also that the board of directors will
be made more responsible.

Once those are accomplished, I suggest the
following:

a. Rebuild confidence in our product.
b. Decentralize the company.
c. Eliminate all departments, activities,

and paperwork not absolutely needed to produce a quality product at a competitive cost to sell at a profit. I recognize that, in accomplishing these, harmonious relations must be maintained with customers, employees, suppliers, government agencies, the general public, and our shareholders.

d. Emphasize long-term profit goals as much as short-term goals.

e. Insist on programs and goals that will result reasonably soon in a series of six or eight news releases announcing exciting accomplishments. This is needed to improve our company image.

f. Reestablish our technological leadership.

g. Diversify.

h. Insist on a professional approach to our store and dealer sales.

i. Launch an aggressive campaign against the ambulance-chasing lawyers who are attempting to destroy us with product claims.

j. Require SMASCO officers and employees to assume their rightful responsibilities and discontinue the promiscuous use of consultants.

k. Zealously guard our trade and technical secrets.

l. Revitalize our personnel and compensation programs to restore employee loyalty and pride.

m. Infuse class into all elements of our company.

n. Reinstall SMASCO on the "best-managed company" list.

The overall program outlined requires that we replace corporate politicians with corporate statesmen. They must not only participate in, but be leaders of, a reindustrialization of America. Government, business, labor, and management must all unite to regain our industrial leadership. Increased productivity in all segments is required to control inflation. Tax incentives for business investment and tax cuts to reduce cost of capital are needed. Energy problems must be neutralized. And do-gooders with outlandish demands will have to be converted to born-again Americans.

For many years, SMASCO enjoyed the type of leadership implied in the objectives set forth above. I'm convinced we can enjoy it again.

John DeLorean wrote the book On a Clear Day You Can See General Motors. We don't want someone to write On a Clear Day You Can't See SMASCO. If we don't put an end to the current management's shell games, Palmer excluded, there may be nothing but a corporate shell remaining. Then no one will be able to see SMASCO on any kind of day.

I. M. Vested

To I. M. Vested

The last memo. The author writes to himself.

1616 Old Mill Road
Clarkton, Illinois
February 28, 1980

Mr. I. M. Vested
1616 Old Mill Road
Clarkton, Illinois

Dear Ian:

The discussion with Fred Ley this morning prompts this letter to myself.

With my normal retirement date just one year away, Fred inquired as to my plans. He indicated another promotion was available if I had more time. Nevertheless, I gave him the decision to retire at sixty-five.

The discussion and decision naturally resulted in many reflections throughout the remainder of the day.

Ian, if you were smart enough to make all the analyses, observations, and predictions as portrayed in all those unsent memos, why didn't your brilliance catapult you into first-tier corporate officership or even into the chief executive officer's chair? What happened? What would you do differently? How would you advise others, particularly young people, entering the business world?

Well, it doesn't require much soul-searching to provide the following answers and advice:

    a. You hated the thought of being a corporate politician and were stubborn

174

enough to believe you could achieve
your goals without entering the rat
race. You thought you had to be a rat to
be in it.

b. You had sold yourself to the family-
controlled management group, but you
were shunned by the succeeding professional managers. They were probably
afraid of you because of your ability to
see through their veneer.

c. You refused to promote yourself at
the expense of someone else. More bla-
tantly stated, you wouldn't knife anyone in the back.

d. You were ahead of the times in believing that we should not expect an indi-
vidual executive's actions as a
businessman to be different from his
personal sense of responsibility to
his family, to society in general, and
to his own conscience.

e. Recognizing the changing trends regarding ethics in business, it shouldn't be
necessary to do anything differently
if you were now at the beginning of
your career.

With such thoughts in mind, you should urge
all competent and dedicated young people to
accept the challenges of American corporate life. The corporations and our nation
need them. The manner in which they accept
and perform the management role will determine
whether American corporations withstand the
onslaught of foreign competitors. It may

quite possibly determine whether our free enterprise system survives.
    I predict that it will.

Notes

I suspect that many readers will have the question, "Why didn't Vested send the memos?" The best answer is in the form of another question. "Is there anyone who has worked for a living who hasn't come home some evenings frustrated, astounded, or infuriated and mentally drafted memos—memos that were never produced in final form and sent?"

SMASCO's management weaknesses became discernible during the late 1960s when the author was in his early fifties. Many corporations were emphasizing youth in management, creating a placement and career-change fear for the older executives. Also, the 1970 economic downturn augmented the reluctance to hazard a change.

With so many happy and proud years of service with SMASCO, the author continued believing, or at least hoping, that corrective measures would appear. The great loyalty to the fine company he had chosen on graduation from college was undoubtedly a primary force that thwarted a change.

The reluctance to change companies was also prompted by the author's conviction that *management makes the difference*. His frequent comment was, "An ice cream stand, a shoe store, or a multinational corporation will succeed or fail depending on its management." He had been closely associated with and involved in several highly successful turnaround situations. He thrived on pride in accomplishment. He chose to endure the pain and hoped to see SMASCO healthy again.

In addition to the above, the author's superiors had rewarded him quite satisfactorily financially until, of course, the last several years when all executives' bonuses were lowered.

Converting some of the mental memos to printed ones and sending them may or may not have placed the author's position with the company in jeopardy. It is believed now that some of the improvements that have been recently made by the new management would have been made earlier if the memos had been sent.